THE CHRISTIAN IMAGE
*STUDIES IN RELIGIOUS ART AND POETRY*

# THE CHRISTIAN IMAGE
## STUDIES IN RELIGIOUS ART AND POETRY

**Justus George Lawler**

Second Impression

Duquesne University Press
Pittsburgh, Pa.

Editions E. Nauwelaerts, Louvain

—also by Justus George Lawler

Towards a Living Tradition (editor)

The Christian Imagination: Studies in Religious Thought

The Catholic Dimension in Higher Education

The Challenge of *Mater Et Magistra* (co-editor)

Nuclear War: The Ethic, The Rhetoric, The Reality

Library of Congress Catalog Card Number 65-19200
© 1966, by DUQUESNE UNIVERSITY

Produced in U.S.A., Computer Typesetting, Inc., Pittsburgh, Pa.

*FOR DONNA*

# CONTENTS

# Foreword

The present studies were written during the course of the last decade. "The Word and the Words" and "Poet, Metaphysician, and the Desire for God," were written in 1962-63. The present publication is the first appearance in print of any of the essays on poetry, though a shorter version of "Poet, Metaphysician, and the Desire for God," appeared in *Spirit As Inquiry: Studies in Honor of Bernard Lonergan* (*Continuum*, Autumn, 1964). The studies on poetry represent fragments of a larger work on Christian poetics, completion of which has had to be periodically postponed under the pressure of less attractive but more insistent projects. The essay on sacred art appeared originally in *Worship* and that on Chagall, in *Thought*. I am grateful to the editors of those journals for permission to use these studies here in a revised form.

I must thank once again my two assistants, Marianne Bankert and Denise Duffy, for their help in preparing this work for publication. I am particularly grateful to the former for sharing with me her rich insights into the poetry of Wallace Stevens. Lastly, I must express my gratitude to Susan Breen and Ellen Arl, who with characteristic generosity, assisted me in a number of tasks relating to this book.

Justus George Lawler

# 1

## The Word and The Words

Discussions on the relation of literature and religion, of poetry and prayer have proved so sterile since the universal discarding of Abbé Bremond's celebrated thesis that religiously minded critics now confine themselves to elaborating parallels between the contents of profane and sacred literature—the adamic type, the Christ-figure, etc. —rather than to exploring similarities of function and form. Yet it is only through this latter undertaking that the essential kinship between the two subjects can be discerned. While one might, for example, be inclined to believe that the nursery rime which relates that "the dish ran away with the spoon" refers to the lance and the chalice, and *a fortiori* to the male and female principles, the deeper significance of these two figures is that they are but one of a great number of ways of imaging forth the fusion of "the one and the many." [1] Similarly, to see in the immersion of the paschal candle in the basin of water, which occurs in the Roman liturgy of Holy Saturday, only a symbol of the consummation of the marriage of heaven and earth is to ignore the archetypal meaning of the act. For this rite, like the recurring use of the sacred number ten and its components—one, three, seven—like the figure of the fountain and the living tree, also represents simply the fundamental effort and only mission of man: to merge the worlds of unity and multiplicity, of spirit and matter.[2]

Now it is only on this most fundamental level that the real bonds between religion and poetry can be discovered. My purpose, therefore is not to discuss the appearance of parallel or derivative themes in sacred and profane literature, but rather to point up the substantive affinities. And I will attempt to do this first by drawing attention to the light that the *infima doctrina* of poetry can cast upon what seems to be exclusively an issue in the *sacra doctrina* of religion.

I

It is a commonplace to affirm that much devotionalism is tinged with sadism, and that Christianity above all has condoned the venting of the most morbid instincts of self-destruction and self-abnegation in the worship of its suffering God. And even Roman Catholic and Anglican liturgists have expressed criticism of the frequent depiction of Christ in a state of agony and pain, on the grounds that the risen Jesus reigns now at the "right hand of the Father" in glory. But if this is so, one must wonder why the religiously inclined seem so obsessed with such devotions as those to "the crowning with thorns," "the scourging at the pillar," etc. Apart from the fact that Christians do adore a person who underwent agony and death in history, and with the most liberal allowance for the possibility that certain ritual acts may be rooted in a kind of mental masochism, it is the contention here that there are other anterior bases for this cult of the suffering God. I am not then concerned now either with aberrant psychic urges or with the doctrinal interpretation of such deaths as that of Adonis or of Christ, but only with another —and I believe more radical—explanation of the historical fact that in every religious tradition there has been a worship of the deity that is always conceived in terms of abasement and spoliation.

Man lives in the world of matter, while being drawn to the world of spirit, in the world of multiplicity and separability while experiencing a longing for the world of unity. And all of man's words have definitions; that is, they are limited and confined because they are rooted primarily in that world of matter which is the domain of the finite, even as spirit is the domain of the infinite. But if man is an "infinite in the finite," as the German philosophers and as poets such as Wordsworth and Browning have explicitly affirmed, it is a contradiction to maintain that he is going to be able to voice his infinity in words which have definitions, which are finite.

When a man speaks an authentic word he is seeking to speak his very selfness. And since he is attempting to exteriorize his interiority, we refer to such speech as an "uttering," an "outering." But most of man's speech is not a true utterance because it is not the attempt to voice his very *being*, to voice what makes him to be a man, but rather it is the enunciation merely of his *doing*, of what makes him to be a thing. *Everyday* talk (by which we mean that speech which is caught up in the world of matter and therefore is essentially *in time*, in the quotidian) functions on the plane of doing, making, or having, that is, on the plane of matter. The plane of matter is the plane of separability, of part outside of part; it is the plane on which subject and object cannot be united. For matter being by definition the principle of multiplicity can never be *one;* similarly matter by being defined as the "all out-

11

side" can never be entered into; it is the thoroughly super-ficial.

All of this is brought out in our syntax: when we say, "I make a kite," or, "I kick the box," in each case we are on the plane of making and doing where subject and object are not *one*. On the other hand, when we speak an authentic word, a true utterance of our "innerance," which proclaims not what we do or have, but what we *are*, then by its very nature as an inner reality, it is spirit, and it immediately brings about that unity which resides only in the domain of spirit. (It is necessary to insert that *being* and *spirit* are here used interchangeably, since what makes me to be what I am is the spirit I am.) In the domain of being, subject and object are dissolved into a oneness, as when we say, "Mary *is* good," or, "The boy *is* happy." Here in the domain of isness, the beginning and the end are the same, and there is no subject and object *as such*, for they reside—at least grammatically—in a perfect reciprocity.[3] And of course there can be no subject and object "as such" because the world of the "as such" is the world of the defined. This perfect reciprocity on the plane of being is what St. Paul calls the "great mystery"[4] in his discussion of marriage in the Epistle to the Ephesians; it is the "great mystery" whether it refers to all earthly lovers seeking union, whether it refers, with St. Paul, to the union of Christ and his church, or whether it refers to what Wallace Stevens terms "the weddings of the soul."[5]

But what then can man do when he seeks to utter the word of unity rather than the word of multiplicity? What must he do when he seeks to truly "outer" his "inness," to express his being? In the strict sense he can "do" nothing, for doing, as we have noted, is always on the plane of matter, of separability. There can be, therefore, no recipe or method or technique or device, since all of these are

12

THE WORD AND THE WORDS

rooted in the world of matter, and thus cannot bring what man most seeks. the plane of spirit and unity. When Hopkins says, "a glance master more may than gaze, gaze out of countenance," [6] he is asserting that no tedious, studied effort, no methodic plodding, that is, no gazing, can assure one of union with the other; it is the immediate encounter, the unplanned and unplanable insight that alone can relate inwardness to inwardness, being to being.

It is the speech of inness man is seeking to outer: as when the Roman liturgy applies to Mary giving birth to Jesus the statement of the Old Testament, "My heart hath uttered a good word." [7] A *good* word is all the heart can utter because the utterance of the heart is the utterance of spirit, of that "being" of which "good" is a manifestation.[8] The speech of matter is the speech which confines and is confined; it is the body-speech which touches only the outside of us, which is limited to limbs (limns) and never reaches "heart." It is therefore not authentic speech but only a kind of ventri-loquism employed by those of whom we crudely but accurately say, "They have more guts than brains," more exteriority than interiority.

One can understand, then, why the doctrine of the "virgin birth" has been preserved by all the major Christian bodies in both East and West. It is a virgin who "utters the good word," for virginity in its radical sense implies simplicity and purity, that is, implies oneness and integrity. Virginity is the state in which interiority is so diffused through matter, that the person is "utterly" one; the word simply flows forth in the speech which we refer to as "fluent." In the Christian tradition, therefore, it is Mary the virgin who conceives in silence the greatest of ideas, and utters in silence the "loudest" of words.

To speak one's true word—and every true word we

13

speak is seeking to be one word because *being* is one—man must move from the plane of doing, making, and having, which is the plane of the disjunctive, and onto that plane of being which is the domain of spirit and of unity. The spirit-word, as we have seen, is the only word that can be truly outered because the matter-word, rooted in the physical, was never innered. Matter has no interiority; it is all outsideness. And the speech of matter, therefore, is the speech which is constrained by precise definitions; whereas the speech of spirit, as all literary critics confirm, is a speech which is striving to express infinition. Hence, to improve on Empson, it may be said that the language of spirit (poetry and prayer) admits of seventy times seven types of ambiguity. The speech of spirit seeks to dissolve all definitions of all words into the one definition of that Logos who is by nature un-definable, who is described as the *Deus ineffabilis*. Spirit-speech seeks to re-ligamentize (the putative and still the aptest cognate of re-ligio) the multiplicity of words so that they are fused to the one Word in which they find their fullest meaning. It would be to go too far afield, and would entail a complete esthetic to show how rime (the bringing of disparate terms into a unity), how rhythm (the unifying of fragmented sonic patterns), alliteration (the abdication of literal meaning in favor of sonic unity), and every poetic mode is seeking to draw all words back to the one Word.

The language of spirit is the true utterance; it is the language of liberty and leisure in which the infinite escapes from the definite, the free from the enslaved; or better, does not escape, but instead converts the density of darkness into light, penetrates by the power of spirit the world of matter, and so is simply diffused out into a oneness with all light, with all spirit. There is no other freedom than to transcend the confines, the limits, and to be one with Being. This is *otium* in the deepest sense, the leisure which liberates and in which man finds himself truly "at ease." It is the contradictory of the world of neg-otium, of uneasiness and unrest in which man carries on the business of doing, making, and having, and in which he is enslaved. For nothing is more enslaved than that which cannot escape from its own confines, from what Milton calls the "darksome house of mortal clay." [10] Thus the supreme transcending of limits is in the act of dying when one is completely separated from his limns. This is the ultimate *otium* when man is utterly liberated and leisured. Thus Keats can speak of "easeful death," and Herbert can find in the letters of Christ's name, IESU, the phrase, "I ease you": [11] a wordplay which is founded on the phrase, "I is you," for, according to the axiom, in God's Isness we fully are: *homo magis Dei quam sui ipsius.* And when Rimbaud says, "Je est un autre," he is, like every poet and every priest, seeking to translate his isness to the isness of others: and this alone is ease. Similarly, the opposite of the wholeness of holiness which ease brings is that state of fragmentation known as dis-ease.

Poetry and prayer, which are both efforts at the uttering of spirit always, then, entail the speaking of the self; by *being* what he is man voices his isness: this is to "deal out that being indoors each one dwells," [13] to cite Hopkins again. It is not to compulsively force one's word out, for to force is to be on the plane of constraint, which is the definition of matter; rather, to "deal out" is to freely and unreflectingly dispense one's being to another. Such is the prayer of the utterly unified person, of the saint, of Francis of Assisi and Father Zossima, and pre-eminently of Christ when he felt a power go out from him: the power was literally exousia, the radiation of his very substance. [14] This is to "speak myself," as Hopkins, again, says, and it is to

15

have a perfect unity between spirit and matter so that "what I *do is* me," so that doing is being, matter is spirit.

By his spirit so fully penetrating his matter that his matter is as it were spiritualized, man restores himself to integrity; he is no longer the fraction drawn two ways, but an integer. Hopkins' term for this spontaneous free outflow of being, "deal," is, then, the Anglo-Saxon counter-part of the term used to refer to the breathing out of God's own Word. The Word is dispensed to man in the new dispensation; no longer is it an action, a *doing* of a multiplicity of ritual observances which is the sign of the alliance as it was in the Old Testament, but it is, as in the New Testament, the uttering of a word: the very Word of God who is the pensée of the Father is dis-pensed in this dispensation.

When man is truly *moved* by his spirit going "out" (that is, literally "ecstatic" and "educated"), when he is truly *touched* by the being outside of him entering into him, when in the reciprocity of being which is experienced only when he is utterly open, that is when he has learned simply "to place no obstacle"[15] in the way of spirit, then he feels himself united with all reality, because all being is one. Both words which I have italicized express the full play of man's spiritual "faculties": because it is the intellect which is "moved" out of the person to embrace the object, and it is the will that is "touched" by the entrance of the object into itself. But this "wholesome," unifying power of the encounter of being is evident even more fully in the domain of the beautiful because the beautiful is a balance between the two polar realities of spirit and matter, of ekstasis and stasis, of universality and concreteness. We therefore speak of the beautiful as something which is "becoming" (*be* representing fulness and perfection; *coming*, emptiness and imperfection) and we refer to God who is all-beautiful not simply as the "immutable," but also as

16

the "ever-changing," that is, as he in whom all things are becoming. This dual tendency which is at once "in" and "out" is the basis for the very notion of in-counter; and it also indicates why in English we may use the word "cleave," which signifies both unity and separation (a joining and a rejoinder), of the intensest love of man and woman.

In the world of matter—which, as we have noted, is the world of prose—doing, making, and having are supreme: in prose the word should have one definition and only one, and we should say exactly what we want. Thus the vices of prose are the virtues of poetry, for the poetic word is ambiguous and admits of many "definitions." Because the world of prose is the world of matter, of the "made," we speak rightly of it as the world of "matter of fact" realities, and in this world truly *actions* speak louder than words." But on the other hand in the world of being, words speak louder than facts; they speak louder by being the contradiction of the world where men do, make, and have; they speak louder by being silent, because silence is to noise as spirit is to matter. And thus one of the earliest poems of Blake explicitly defines poetry as speaking silence.[16]

The world of infinition is the world of interiority, just as the world of definition is the world of exteriority. If man is going to voice a true utterance, he must go from the in to the outer in order that the outer may enter in. He must speak not in empty declamation, nor in the supremely material speech of the imperative shout. Rather he must speak the "under-standing" speech, the speech which is *under the static* material envelope. Speech-in-understanding, then, is spirit-speech; it is the speech which voices the spirit under the matter and which is, therefore, always true to its "subject matter." The imperative speech is only noise

17

and expresses only the material world of stasis, of absolute impermeability: it is also what we usually refer to exasperatedly as "so much static."

This is why the mood of prayer and poetry is the subjunctive. It is the mood in which something is cast under something else, in which spirit is cast under matter, interiority under exteriority. On the other hand, matter-speech, prose, is always in the indicative; it is the speech of people who "talk at" another, and who never utter their own interiority nor touch the interiority of another. Matter-speech, therefore, is descriptive speech which covers only the outsides of things, as one would describe a circle. Whereas spirit-speech literally "beggars description."

Similarly the indicative is the mood of the world of matter-of-fact-thingness; it is the mood in which one is not united with the other, but in which the other is beyond one, and is only to be indicated, to be pointed at. It is the speech which treats the sacred other as a mere object, and for this reason in our lessoning of children, we tell them "never point at people": things are to be pointed at, indicated with our index finger, but persons are to be touched interiorly through the subjunctive. And man's very nature is that he is a "perhaps," an "able to be" subjunctive creature. This is why the world which contradicts the world of the indicative where we "can see for ourselves," is the spirit world where things only "seem"; for see is to seem as the indicative is to the subjunctive.

People who live on the indicative, who live as objects, have no meaning in themselves: they are only "pointers." Such people approach all reality on the objective plane, and they are therefore, as we commonly say, people who are "shallow" or "superficial" because they are all outsideness and exteriority. They are the very people of whom one says that he couldn't "get through" to them. He cannot "influence" them because there is no "in" into which he can flow; there is only an outside which sheds all true words. The people to whom one cannot get through are the dense, imprisoned in the dens of their own matter, and ever busy about many things. The light of the countenance of being is not signed upon them; it has been extinguished, and one thinks of them as being "dull" or "thick"—both terms which denominate matter. Such people "don't *mean* anything to us," and they cannot interest us because there is no inter-esse, no exchange of being; only an exchange of matter, or better—because matter cannot be exchanged since it is the principle of incommunicability—there is no "exchange" at all: there is only an abrasion, a colliding, or, as common speech discloses, "two bumps on a log." And for such people the "other" is always the enemy because the other is always seen in the accusative. Similarly, their own self is objectified so that not only are they "afraid" of themselves, but they cannot utter the subjunctive word which transcends matter: "I wish I were." The word which they speak is always the acquisitive and imperative accusative: "*Me* first."

Since man is, and since matter exists for spirit, the only realities that truly inter-est him, that is, that "fit" him (relate to him) and make him happy, are being and Being. In the Christian conception, the creature's being is a participation in the supreme being of the Godhead ("I am who am"), and it is this sharing in being which engenders relationships ("a lying-down-together") and which creates what we call "mutual inter-ests." Since "God is light," he is according to Hopkins the source of all those "rich beams" that "interest our eyes." Thus to be closed to being is—as Hopkins says in a brilliant blending of the notions of light and being—to be "beamblind,"[17] that is, blind to the be-amness, to the very isness of God. And one would like

19

to think that the young Yeats, when he was looking at the little artificial fountain of the one and the many and meditating "The Lake Isle of Innisfree," realized for a moment that true paradise is found in the "bee-loud glade."

But as we have observed already, because being transcends the plane of doing, making, and having, there can be no way or method or recipe for attaining happiness in this union of being; there is literally nothing man can do; he can only *be*, and his isness will encounter the isness of another; and since isness says unity, he is necessarily one with the other. This is the *admirabile commercium*,[18] the "extraordinary exchange" in which being and being are joined.

For this reason Milton, when he was attempting to put aside the poetry of the physical and of the world of multiplicity—that is, the poetry of "L'Allegro" and *Comus*—described the muse of his anticipated spiritual poem—*Paradise Lost*—as the perfect fusion of opposites and as "commercing with the skies":[19]

> *Come*, but *keep* thy wonted state,
> With *even step*, and *musing gait*,
> And looks commercing with the skies,
> Thy *rapt* soul *sitting* in thine eyes.

All exchanges on heaven and earth are named after this exchange;[20] it is therefore the contradictory of the "exchange of stock" which takes place in the world of *negotium*, in the world of uneasiness and enslavement. Hence John Donne describes carnal love, the love necessarily limited to limbs, as "small change,"[21] by contrast to the infinite richness of the intercourse of spirit. Every exchange of stock requires the coinage of money which buys only the dis-ease of business, the abrasion and rebuffing of the other

—and so it is never possible to succeed in business without really trying, for only the world of otium, the contradiction of negotium, is the world where one need never try.

One can descry the whole evolution—or better, atrophy —of Tennyson's art in his rejection of the currency of otium for the currency of negotium—in his flight from the twi-lit land of the lotos-eating poets, from the tower of Shalott, from the wedding with Aurora, from the palace of art, from the mountain height, and down to the cities of business, down to Camelot, to the dim fields, to the cottage in the vale, and to the exchange of stock.[22] The climax of this descent from the *admirabile commercium* to mere commerce takes place in that monstrous parody of poetry and paean to prose when Tennyson said he[23]

> Saw the heavens fill with commerce, argosies of magic sails,
> [sales?]
> Pilots of the purple twilight, dropping down with costly bales;
> Heard the heavens fill with shouting, and there rained a ghastly blue. . . .

Not Wordsworth coining ecclesiastical sonnets to pay for the riband to stick in his coat, not Arnold hectoring the philistines so sold his muse for such a handful of silver as did Victoria's laureate. For the true *admirabile commercium* does not take place in the stock exchange; it takes place in the spirit exchange, where all commodities are too dear to purchase, where nothing can ever be possessed or had, where there is no satis-faction, and where everything else except the currency of poetry and prayer, coined by the spirit, is counterfeit.

Just as on the plane of matter, "actions speak louder than words," so too, in the world of negotium, "money talks." It is the man of business who exclaims, "I'll buy that," when he "takes one's meaning"; and it is on the stock

21

exchange that one is told, "put your money where your mouth is," or is offered, "a penny for your thoughts." This identification of money and speech is a commonplace: both are coined, minted, and put into currency; words are "golden," "bankrupt," "sterling," "counterfeit," "spent," "brokers."[24] The parallel, of course, stems from the viability and the representative character of both; but on a more elementary level it derives from a common reference to the mouth, so that even today money is referred to as "dough" or "bread," phrases like "eat one's words" remain current, and poets like Stevens can affirm that man "lives on the bread of faithful speech"[25]—a text with obvious scriptural overtones.

In an exegesis which would probably be repugnant to the twentieth-century mind, Léon Bloy explained the commercial genius of the Jewish people as the result of their losing the Word of God and their retaining only its visible type, money.[26] The basis of this explanation was the verse of the Psalm (11:7), "The *words* of the Lord, pure words, are *silver* tried by fire." Whatever Bloy's idiosyncratic historical interpretation, the passage can be recognized as referring to the crucible of the Godhead in which the Word was expressed from all eternity; and it is noteworthy that this Word was begotten after the same manner in which —as I shall show in Part Two—the poetic tradition envisions the imagination's engendering of a poem. There is a certain trans-logical harmony in the fact, then, that a man professionally committed to the world of insurance, interest, brokerage, premiums, etc., should be the greatest American poet of this century, and that he should declare: "Money is a kind of poetry."[27] It is a kind of poetry only because the finite is a kind of infinite and the poem is a kind of sacrament. But this "kind of" like the definition of man as "kind of" everything (*quodammodo omnia*) makes literally "all the difference in the world," for it makes the difference between matter and spirit.

Since there is nothing one can do to attain spirit, nothing one can buy or sell, there are no rules to follow, no techniques or methods which will guarantee union with another: we have "rules of thumb" only for "matters at hand." One cannot make himself love another or pray to God, or marvel at a truth. As Wallace Stevens says of these occurrencies, which come from fluency in that true speech which Keats calls our "mother tongue," they "occur as they occur."[28] Because spirit is the principle of absolute freedom—one can always pre-dict matter, one can only prophesy spirit[29] —the union with another, the mergence of being and being, is rightly regarded as an *accident*, as a pure *chance*. Both terms are variations of "cadere" and so a person always speaks of the encounter with being, he always speaks of the intense spiritual event, as something that "befell" him, and he may talk with great accuracy of "falling in" love. Because this encounter with being is every philosopher's definition of happiness, anything which *befalls* man is a happening, and every happening is happiness, even as the *glücklich* are always lucky and the lucky are always happy. These encounters are the most intense experiences of this life; only "death's intenser" as Keats said, because in death man is completely *uttered*, completely undefined in what Keats, again, with rigorous precision refers to as "easeful death."[30]

To talk about this happiness when it happens requires a fluency beyond that of prose. To speak the interior experience man needs a speech which dissolves the indicative and accusative restraints and transcends the world of matter of fact. To voice this trans-indicative, there is no other mood than the subjunctive. To say, "I wish I were," is to make an affirmation that contradicts the universe of *facta*,

23

of doing, making, and having. To voice the in-counter of being one must contradict the indicative: to speak spirit one must be silent in matter. These "contradictations" are the motive for metaphor and reason of analogy. The man in love refers to his beloved by precisely those terms that indicate what she is not. He does not express his love to a 5′ 3″, 110 lb., brown-haired, good-cooking, etc., woman. He does not do so because this is exactly what in the world of matter of fact she is, and his love does not reside in that world. She is to him, "baby," "honey," "sweet," etc.. He is driven to tell lies in the world of matter if he is going to speak truths in the world of spirit.

This, then is the center of the original problem: there is a devotion to the suffering God—apart from whatever theological-historical reasons—as the "worm and no man"[31] because such terms provide man with the best mode for realizing the infinite spirit of the deity. Similarly there is a devotion in the Christian tradition to the infant Jesus because infanthood is the one condition that best expresses the contradictory of the deity as the "immortal king of ages." Thus one of the most intense utterances of the praying spirit is, "Jesus condemned to death, have mercy on us." That paradox contains the whole of the metaphoric thrust and of what the poet says:[32]

> Welcome, all wonders in one sight.
> Eternity shut in a span.
> Summer in winter, day in night
> Heaven in earth, and God in man.
> Great little one whose all-embracing birth
> Lifts earth to heaven, stoops heaven to earth.

And all of the above reflections are but a gloss on the axiom that the "simple can be imitated only by the compound,"[33] and on the poet's and mystic's insight that God is "dark with excessive bright."[34]

## II

With this by way of prelude we are in a position to grasp more fully the relationship of poetry and prayer, or of "literature" and "theology." For both priest and poet are seeking consciously—as every man is attempting implicitly—to fuse spirit and matter, the priest successfully in the sacrament, the poet defectively in the poem. Therefore it is false to say that "poems are made by fools like me, but only God can make a tree," since the sacrament is the only authentic poem because it is the only authentic extension of the God in whom "spirit" and "matter," existence and essence are absolutely one. It is the agony and frustration of the poet that while he is seeking to restore man to what Blake called the "world of innocence," that is to the world in which subject and object, lion and lamb, were one, he must always fail; while the priest as the agent of the only *word* which was truly made *flesh* always succeeds. Both priest and poet are pontiffs, but the bridging of the gap between spirit and matter, which the priest achieves, remains for the poet only an elusive dream: "C'est vrai, c'est à l'Éden que je songeais,"[35] says Rimbaud.

The sin of Eve in the biblical story was not that she sought to be as God, "knowing good and evil"; it was that she sought to fulfill this destiny through a poem rather than through a sacrament. Man becomes God—to paraphrase St. Augustine—only by God becoming man. To "know good and evil," as the very phrase itself indicates, is to fuse contradictories, to fuse being and non-being, spirit and matter,[36] in the perfect poem that only God *is*.

25

But Eve, as an image of God, experienced the strain of these polar attractions, and therefore sought to be not the image, but the reality. She succumbed to the temptation of every poet: to believe that the poem really works what it says, that the shadow is the truth, that the spheroid fruit of the tree of the one and the many—Stevens' "jar in Tennessee," Coleridge's "pleasure dome," Keats' "Grecian Urn," MacLeish's "globed fruit"—truly links together the ultimate extremes of things, truly is the alpha and omega.

Because Eve mistook the *shadow* for the substance, the English poets have always played on her name and envisioned her as the "evening maiden." But she is the eve-woman, in a deeper sense, because it is only in twilight that the poem is wrought, it is only in the two lights of night and day, in the fusion of these extremes, that the poem dwells. Poetry is always achieved not by the light of the burning sun—"We shrink from the light of primary noon,"[37] as Stevens says—nor in the utter darkness, but in the light of the sun as reflected from the dark opacous moon, that is, in the light which blends black and white. Eve the poet, and the poet is every man in his purest natural state, dwells in the chiasm where two worlds intersect. And so she stands in Eden,[38]

> Wondering, listening,
> Listening, wondering.

She is the true Proserpine who resides in both worlds—in the "best of dark and bright"—and who is also therefore described by Milton chiasmically:[39]

> Not that fair field
> Of Enna, where Proserpine *gathering flowers*
> Herself a fairer *flower* by gloomy Dis

> Was *gathered*, which cost Ceres all that pain
> To seek her through the world. . . .

The last clause describes the eternal plodding quest of Demeter for that lost childhood when spirit and matter seemed perfectly blended.[40] And all men are necessarily following in her path, seeking to be initiated into the new Eleusinian mysteries so that they can glean from the world of multiplicity the ancient principle of unity. Ceres is the guide and matrix of man's exiled state;[41] she is a symbol of the quest "amid the alien corn" for that reality which will blend the worlds of matter and spirit, of "reaping and singing"; and so she leads all men to pursue with the poet-king "the chaffy grain beneath the thresher's flail" which is to be ground into the sacramental communion loaf, into that loaf which is not "unkneaded doughbaked prose," nor even the poet's ginger-bread boy, but the "bread of life" which truly joins heaven to earth, which truly merges all contradictories.[42] Our fathers did feast on poems in the desert, but we are meant to consume the archetypal sacrament. And as Hopkins says, this bread which fuses the high and the low, the heavenly and the earthly, is Christ:[44]

> . . . I lift *up* heart, eyes,
> *Down* all that glory in the heavens to glean our Saviour.

We invariably think of the world of matter as the plane of the horizontal and the world of spirit as the plane of the vertical, with the combination of the two forces generating the oblique or slanted line. Thus revelation, or better, "mediation" between spirit and matter, between heaven and earth, between the vertical and the horizontal, takes place on the slopes of mountains, as at Sinai or the Mount of the Beatitudes, or Tabor and Calvary; so, too, the

27

poem which is seeking to blend all extremes is born, according to Coleridge, on "the chasm which slanted," and its guiding spirit is the muse of whom Keats said, "sideways would she lean."[45] But the more accurate figure for the line which is drawn both to the vertical and the horizontal is the arabesque. It is this serpentine line which Coleridge used to suggest the drift of poetry—"Five miles meandering with a mazy motion"—and T. E. Hulme rightly described as snake-like.[46] For this reason in the biblical tradition, the "light bearer" who is the "prince of darkness," when he came to tempt Eve took the form of a serpent whom Milton characterized as moving on the slant, "with tract oblique." Milton goes on to describe him as colored in "verdant gold," [47] that is, in the colors of spirit-matter, for green and blue are the colors of spirit, even as red and yellow are the colors of matter.[48]

And therefore the making of metaphor, according to Stevens, requires the "hammer of red and blue" in the in-between seasons of spring and autumn when we "shrink from the light of primary noon."[49] What Yeats called "the prosaic light of day,"[50] destroys all poetry, all merging of dualities, as the legend of the hyacinth indicates: for it is the blending of the red and blue (the purple patches) that is undone when Hyacinth the pride of Spartan land is slain by the disc of the sun. Similarly Phyllis (the blending of yellow and blue) flees from Cleveland's garden of poetry and abandons her twi-lit state to the light of prose:[51]

> and (lest her stay
> Should wed October unto May;
> And as her beauty caused a spring
> Devotion might an autumn bring)
> Withdrew her beams, yet made no night,
> But left the sun her curate-light.

Finally this interplay of the colors of spirit (blue, green) and matter (red, yellow) serves to explain why the feast of Christmas, the feast of spirit becoming matter, of Word becoming flesh, is celebrated with green and red, and why the incarnate Christ, the fusion of blue and red, is seen by Donne as "purple," and by Hopkins as "very violet sweet."[52]

In the Christian perspective the true bond between heaven and earth is the arabesque which is Christ; and Christ himself explained Moses' raising of the serpent on the cross in the desert as a prototype of his being raised on the chiasm of Calvary.[53] The poem, then, is to sacrament as the serpent in the Old Testament, or even the intertwined serpents of Mercury, is to Christ. And no one will ever know whether Coleridge when he had his mariner saved by the sight of the paradoxic water snakes—a sight which ultimately allowed him to bless *"all* things, both *great* and *small"*[54]—was referring to the power of Christ or of poetry; whether, that is, Coleridge was thinking of the poem as possessing a sacramental power— "to know *good* and *evil"*—or whether he was merely imaging forth its fictive fusioning power in terms similar to those of Keats (the chameleon) and Thomas Browne (the amphibian).[55] But one does know why Henry Vaughan could describe man in relation to Christ, poem in relation to sacrament, as a "glow-worm";[56] and one suspects one knows why Patrick the true bishop had to drive the poems out of Ireland before he could preach the sacraments.[57]

The Old Testament in relation to the New Testament may be considered in one or another of the basic polar relations of matter to spirit, of prose to poetry, of drama to lyric, of poem to sacrament. It is for this reason that we think of the Old Testament as pre-eminently a "history," as being essentially caught up in that world which Aristotle defined as inferior to poetry because it is rooted in contingency and pragma, that is, in matter. There is no need to enter into the Cullmann-Bultmann debate over whether the *heilsgeschichtliche* perspective is valid for the New Testament; it is necessary only to note that the fundamental temporality, or better "temporariness," of the Old Testament is completed in the New Testament through Christ who comes in the "fulness of time." Similarily, as noted in Part I, the relation of ten commandments to one commandment, the relation of the multiplicity of ritual observances to the single law which Christ preached, is the relation of matter to spirit. For this reason the sign of the covenant in the Old Testament is the rainbow, is that refracted broken light which in the New Testament becomes the unified brilliance that conquers the darkness.

Nor is it surprising, then, that the punishment inflicted upon man after the destruction of the tower of Babel is the intensification of that multiplicity and separability which had been imposed on Adam and Eve in the garden. The tower of Babel is an image not only of the attempt of man to link heaven and earth by his own efforts, it also symbolizes that Odyssean urge which everyman, and above all the poet, experiences to scale the seven storey mountain by his own power—an attempt, as Dante relates in Canto 26 of *Inferno*, which brings down the wrath of the Trinity: *Tre volte* il fe girar con tutte l'acque. . . . No poetic towers can reach as "high as that": they are predestined to be only the "broken column" of Eliot, the "round squat turret" of Browning,[58] and the tower which Yeats in his old age recognized as having failed to blend the active and contemplative lives.[59] Every tower is overthrown as every poet's moment of light once again succumbs to the "still sad messengers of gray,"[60] and he experiences the burthen of the mystery which weighs down his craft: every "lucid" glimpse (the meaning of "Lycidas" and his death) becomes smothered in the darkness because the muse of every poem is that Eve-figure of Wordsworth —Lucy: whose surname is Gray.

In this architectural context, then, the poet by contrast to the priest is a kind of "freemason" who, "with the ferrel of his stick trying the mortar's temper,"[61] seeks to build the "pleasure dome in air," and inevitably fails because he lacks that keystone of the arch which, according to St. Paul, is Christ.[62] The tower of Babel symbolizes the impossibility of any poem realizing what only the sacrament achieves. Therefore in *Genesis* after Babel the definitions of things were so increased that all unity was further impaired; whereas, in the New Testament, through the sacrament of the Word, the linguistic barriers were so dissolved that—as the *Acts* narrate with primitive wonderment—men of all nations were united through the sermon which Peter uttered at the first Pentecost:[63]

And how have we heard, every man our own tongue wherein we were born? Parthians and Medes and Elamites and inhabitants of Mesopotamia, Judea, and Cappadocia, Pontus and Asia, Phrygia and Pamphylia, Egypt, and the parts of Libya about Cyrene, and strangers of Rome, Jews also, and proselytes, Cretes, and Arabians: we have heard them speak in our own tongues the wonderful works of God. And they were all astonished, and wondered, saying one to another: what meaneth this?

An equally apt symbol of Old Testament salvation is Jacob's ladder because it represents that world of matter, of plodding step by step, part outside of part, from beginning to end, from alpha to omega. Jacob's ladder, then, is like the drama which in Aristotle's conception must have

31

an explicit *beginning, middle,* and *end;* or, it is like that rational *process*—or better, "procession," in which we pedestrianly plod along the (dis)course of reason—the syllogism, through which we laboriously move from *premise* to *middle* term to *conclusion*: a "conclusion" which, by the very fact that it is the *end,* never gives us what we are really seeking. For, as Cardinal Newman observed, what we want is the beginning with the end, the alpha with the omega; or, as Coleridge said of the ideal poem, "the snake with its tail in its mouth."[64]

On the other hand, the New Testament is like the lyric —man is bid to "lift up his heart"—in which the metaphor immediately works what it says. Through Christ who is Word made flesh, God *is* man and man *is* God, alpha *is* omega and omega *is* alpha. This explains why the Old Testament, relatively speaking, represents a religion of gloom—the darkness of matter has not yet been overcome; the New Testament is the good tidings that bring light and peace: that bring the metaphor which really compacts what is *in excelsis* and what is *in terra.* The "valleys are exalted and the mountains and hills made low" in a peace which "surpasses understanding,"[65] which surpasses all syllogistic and rational categories. For as Blake says,[66]

I come in self-annihilation and the grandeur of inspiration
To cast off rational demonstration by faith in the Savior.

In the New Testament the mediator between heaven and earth is not the plodding rational exercise, the "business about many things," the laborious climbing of the ladder of being, but it is the very being of God. The only word which can achieve the metaphor, "man *is* God," is the Word of God. And so in the New Testament the religion of *otium,* of freedom of spirit is inaugurated, and the religion of slavery to matter—of the bondsman, to which St. Paul referred[67]—and of fear, is at an end. The symbol of this happy union of contingent and absolute being is the rending of the veil of the temple, the dissolution of all "fronts" and barriers, at that moment when on the slopes of Golgotha the chiasm is consummated.

Although the poem seems to give us entrance into the promised land, seems to break down what St. Paul calls "the wall of separation,"[67] it really fails. That figure of the poem which Coleridge envisions as the only mediator around whom we are to weave the three-fold circle of Hermes Trismegistus—[69]

> For he on honey-dew hath fed
> And drunk the milk of Paradise

—this figure does not give us the real Paradise, but only the sham "Mount Abora" of which Milton disdainfully says, "by some supposed true Paradise."[70] And so we are driven to recognize the Kubla-Khan figure as only another "unshaven agent who returned to the camp," and who could not lead us to the "open wishing well."[71]

Man does not find peace in the forerunners and types of Christ, in the bearded prophet's words; he finds peace only in the sacraments of the Word. The entrance to the true promised land can be attained not by any token offerings of poems, nor by any coinage of man's speech, but only by the currency which God the Father mints—velociter *currit* sermo ejus[72]—only by the Word which "reaches from end to end and draws all things to it strongly and sweetly."[73] In this religious conception, it is by the coining of the suffering Christ that man is redeemed out of the pawnshop of Satan, for as Merton says, tears are coins.[74] Thus every poetic word is only the counterfeit of the sacramental word, even as, according to Jeffers, every man is "only the ape of God."[75]

Even though the poem-figure of Kubla Khan "on honey-dew hath fed," (that is, has been consecrated a kind of prophet and priest by that holy anointing which makes his speech "unctuous") he cannot give that true golden fleece of which the "dewy fleece" of Gideon was a type. Instead he can only proffer a fleeting glimpse of the things of this world momentarily transmuted into the things of the other world:[76]

> As I lay down in the grass, I observed the glittering silver line on the ridge of the backs of the sheep, owing to their situation respecting the sun, which made them look beautiful, but with something of strangeness, like animals of another kind, as if belonging to a more splendid world.

But this is not the "fleece of beauty"[77] man is seeking; for the vision fades and the sheep which had been mistaken for the lamb of God becomes only the golden calf, the mimic of Jehovah and fragmented echo of his Word. When the shades of the prison house close about the poet, he recognizes that he is not "nature's priest," and he is compelled to say of himself and of every poet that "by our own spirits are we deified."[78] If the poet honestly faces this failure, if he realizes that what he has wrought is not "a god, but *as a god might be*,"[79] then he must either despair —passionately like Yeats or stoically like Stevens—or he must seek to be deified by *another's* spirit rather than by his own. In the latter event he will cease to be the creator of the "artifice of eternity," of "glass men" who "dewily cry" and of "supreme fictions" that hint at the Word without delivering him—"And whence they came and whither they shall go the dew upon their feet shall manifest"—and he must seek to become what Milton thought himself to be: the consecrated maker not of fictions, but of sacraments which truly shall "fetch the age of gold."[80]

"How beautiful are the feet of those who preach the gospel of peace" is the prophecy Milton was thinking of when he prayed, "But let my due feet never fail to walk the studious cloister's pale."[81] And it is to this anointing dew that another Puritan poet is alluding when he describes the Old Testament dew—the dew of poetry—as a type of that dew which in the New Testament shall "drop down and the earth bud a savior": [82]

> Such did the manna's sacred dew distill;
> White and entire, though congealed and chill:
> Congealed on earth; but does dissolving run
> Into the glories of the *almighty sun*.

But this sacramental dew is not the word of the poet, but the Word of God:[83]

> Then Jesus said to them: Amen, amen I say to you; Moses gave you not bread from heaven, but my Father giveth you the true bread from heaven. For the bread of God is that which cometh down from heaven, and giveth life to the world. They said therefore unto him: Lord give us always this bread. And Jesus said to them: I am the bread of life.

The poet who, like Stevens, is driven to affirm "that final belief/Must be in a fiction"[84] is worshiping at an empty tomb, as Stevens himself was heroic enough to testify. He is coining not the true currency of the Word, but only forgeries; and like the first forger, Aaron, he is hammering out on the anvil of his spirit only another golden calf, only another "self-born mocker of man's enterprise."[85]

> The ruddy temper, the hammer
> Of red and blue, the hard sound—
> Steel against intimation, the sharp flash. . . .

Thus for Stevens are supreme fictions made;[86] and the poet is seen not as the divine "alchemist," the authentic blacksmith, but only as the "sleight-of-hand man." This is the poet who cannot become the priest: as Wordsworth knew, it is the poet as "tinker":[87]

> Down he sits; his brows he knits;
> Then his hammer he rouzes;
> Batter! Batter! Batter!
> He begins to clatter.

Wallace Stevens himself recognized such poetry is only "the heaving speech of air . . . sound alone."[88] For the consecrated poet like Milton, and for the religious man in general, there is no sacramental act here, there is only a ritual gesture to the serpentine Satan-figure. For this reason Milton explicitly compares the first poet-alchemist, Vulcan the blacksmith god, to Lucifer building the palace of artifice.[89] One understands, too, why Blake who esteemed Milton above all poets would have intimated that it is only the divine hand that could wield the hammer which would truly fuse all opposites:[90]

> What the hammer? What the chain?
> In what furnace was thy brain?
> What the anvil? What dread grasp
> Dare its deadly terrors clasp!

Only by the "finger of God" could the tiger in the forests of the night be drawn together with the lamb of innocence.

36

The making of metaphor ought to bring us, as Stevens says, the "life that is fluent in even the wintriest bronze,"[91] the mobile in the immobile, that is, the spirit in the matter. But it was Browning above all English poets who explored in this making of metaphor the parallel between the poetic mission and that of Moses in drawing forth fluency from the stone in the desert:[92]

> He who smites the rock and spreads the water,
> Bidding drink and live a crowd beneath him,
> Even he, the minute makes immortal,
> Proves, perchance, but mortal in the minute,

From the religious point of view, Moses and every poet seeking the promised land find their meaning and fulfillment only in that figure who "out of the very stones is able to raise up children of Abraham," and who described himself as the "living water,"[93] that is, only in the sacramental Word. And for these sacraments there is no magic wand, no serpentine Mosaic staff, no instrumental cause, since God acts as the joiner of heaven and earth, as the fuser of the mobile and the immobile simply by the power of Word.

With one exception all poets are, like Moses, mere stammerers when compared to the fluent makers of sacraments. That one exception is the poet who knew he would not hesitate as Moses did when striking the rock with the rod of his art. It is this protestant poet who believed that his poem was the vehicle of the "two-edged"[94] word of God, and that, as such, it would put an end both to all lesser poems, to all "lean and flashy songs" which feed the spirit with deceptions, and to all sham sacraments confected by the omnivorous papist priests. Speaking of such false shepherds and pontiffs, Milton wrote, in one of the most misunderstood passages in our literature:[95]

> And when they list, their lean and flashy songs
> Grate on their scrannel pipes of wretched straw.
> The hungry sheep look up, and are not fed,
> . . . .
> Besides what the grim wolf with privy paw
> Daily devours apace, and nothing said;
> But that two-handed engine at the door
> Stands ready to smite once, and smite no more.

When Milton said that in Christ "all his Father shone/Substantially expressed," he did so knowing that it was his own poetic sacramental mission to "express Thee unblamed."[96] And thus the relationship of *Paradise Lost* to the "two-edged sword" which is the Word of God is the relationship—in non-protestant terms—of the sacrament to Christ.

But only by the making of the ultimate metaphor can matter embrace spirit; only by life conquering death can the lion and the lamb lie down together. Christ, then, is the true poem, the pantokrator, who "draws all things unto himself"[97] on the chiasm of Golgotha. He above all other metaphors is the "*vital, fatal,* arrogant, dominant X." He is the fusion of life and death, spirit and matter, in the supremely *mysterious* act: for X stands not only for the intersection of extremities, but also for the utterly "unknown." It is this "X," this mystery man seeks, as Stevens says, not "the A B C of being,"[98] not the abecedarian folly of the masonic ritualist or the scholastic rationalist. This is why man delights in "falling in" love, and does not find any delight in the planned and plotted methodic devising of techniques for "loving," why he delights in leaping the gap from subject to object, not in the pedestrian discourse of reason. The making of metaphor is an exercise of being; the making of the perfect metaphor is the act of supreme being—all else is supreme fiction.

Therefore every poet seeking to give us the experience of being distends the poles of his paradox as far as possible. For poetry, as Allen Tate maintains, is a construct of tension; or better, it is a construct of the intension of spirit and the extension of matter in a tension which cancels all "in" and "out." Poetry requires what Tennyson, in a rare insight, calls "the tender grace"[99] which draws together the ultimate extremes of things. That metaphor which is, in Donne's word, "slack,"[100] gives no experience of the power of being. Thus to say, "man is an animal" is to make a metaphor in which the poles are "too near, too clear,"[101] and in which therefore there is little "tenderness." But to say, for example, with Rupert Brooke that "Love is a flame"[102] is to bring antipodes together into a grammatical oneness and to acquire the "tenderest truth."[103] (It should not have to be emphasized now that the only ground of metaphor is the fact that in the mind of God, in the *coincidentia oppositorum*, all extremes as all words are one.) Since for man in his everyday experience the existence of spirit and matter as such is rarely recognized directly, all poets have seen the supreme metaphor in the fusing of life and death. Thus the ancient mariner, who—as Robert Penn Warren showed in a cardinal essay—stands for poetry, is possessed by "life-in-death"; similarly every poet asks with Browning's pontiff ordering his tomb, "Do I live, am I dead?" And what we derive from Tennyson's "idle tears" (the tears of *otium*, ease) is simply, "O death in life."[104]

To truly fuse all opposites life must really enter into death. Then after having passed through "easeful death" man shall be able to sing "of summer in full throated

**39**

ease";[105] he shall be one with God, and shall be, as Donne says, made his "music."[106] He shall then have transcended all metaphors, all twilight states; the lead of "de-spair," of duality, shall be transformed into the gold of "spare," of unity.[107] When like Hyperion man is utterly unlimned,[108] when like Blake's chimney sweepers he shall have put off all the "soots" of this world, then there shall be no more definitions. Then will the " 'weep! 'weep! 'weep!'"[109] of the world of negotium be transmuted into the "sweep! sweep! sweep!" of the world of true otium as he "sweeps the strings"[110] of the eternal diapason. After death man is no longer in the realm of metaphor, he is no longer in the dubious in-between seasons of this world: "You like it [metaphor] under the trees in autumn . . . in the same way, you are happy in spring."[111] Whereas, to sing in "full throated ease" is to sing in the summer season when all is summed, in the season which as Donne says in an outrageously effective pun, is "wholesomer"[112] for us because we have left the world of dis-ease. Then man shall "wash in a river and shine in the sun" of spirit.

It is only when man passes beyond the final definitions through death that the metaphor achieves what it affirms, and is therefore no longer metaphor, but oneness. For this reason the sacrament of baptism, which in this world is the true poem truly bringing new life, the true "Sunday bath," is compared by St. Paul to a death.[113] In the present life it is this ritual entombment in the dense waters—symbolized by Eastern Christians and by pentecostal groups in descent and submersion in the pool of water—that alone brings a fusion of spirit and matter, and that sacramentally perfects all failing poetic efforts. This is why the Church Fathers called baptism *photismos*,[114] an illumination in which not figuratively but *really* "the heavy and the weary weight of all this unintelligible world is *lightened*,"[115] and why in the Roman liturgy the Sunday after the baptismal day is called *dominica in albis*; for on this day the marriage garment of the "weddings of the soul" is finally put on; the return from experience to innocence, from *negotium* to *otium*, is symbolized by putting off all business soots.

Only through death can this fulfillment of every earthly metaphor be realized. And that is why the following much-criticized lines of Keats—criticized for their banality by rationalist critics—contain the most basic of ontological truths:[116]

> "Beauty is truth, truth beauty"—that is all
> Ye know on earth, and all ye need to know.

What man seeks is to fuse opposites, in this instance, "beauty" and "truth"; and in the poem, at least grammatically and structurally, the fusion does seem to take place. "Beauty *is* truth," the poet affirms, and reinforces the affirmation by the chiasmic structure of the two pairs: "*Beauty* is *truth, truth beauty*." To fuse opposites in a true "solution sweet" is to bring them closer and closer together until they are one. The direction of Keats' statement is from three terms to two terms, that is, from some separation to a closer kinship; but to go from three to two to *one*—which is the real goal—is impossible in this world. Hence the break: "Beauty is truth, truth beauty—." To merge "truth-beauty" into an absolute oneness requires the leaping of that gap; it requires the greatest of all of "one's grand flights"[117] beyond this world of separability and into the other world of unity. Thus "all we know *on earth*" is precisely that we can bring opposites metaphorically together in a kind of juxtaposition; but we cannot fuse them into a real oneness, except through the ritual death of sacramental baptism, or through actual physical death.

41

# 2

## Towards a Poetic of the Word

I SUPPOSE, since we are all of us more or less professionally committed to listening to sermons, it might be ad-
visable, after the example of homilists, to give a "text" to
these remarks.[1] The chapter and verse are from Gibbon's
*Journal*, under the date, October 3, 1762, where the his-
torian wrote of Longinus' treatise *On the Sublime*:[2]

> Till now, I was acquainted only with two ways of criticizing
> a beautiful passage: the one, to show by an exact anatomy of
> it, the distinct beauties of it, and from whence they sprung;
> the other, an idle exclamation, or a general encomium, which
> leaves nothing behind it. Longinus has shown me that there is
> a third. He tells me his own feelings upon reading it; and tells
> them with such energy that he communicates them. I almost
> doubt which is the most sublime, Homer's battle of the gods,
> or Longinus's apostrophe to Terentianus upon it.

This justly famous passage is significant because it suggests
a way out of the impasse, out of the dilemma, which has
stymied or inhibited much criticism from the Greeks to
the present day. Possibly one should not speak of criticism
as such, because these comments are concerned not so
much with evaluating works of art as with communicating

their significance to others. The issue, though tangentially critical, is fundamentally, for present purposes, a pedagogical one, and is related to the broader and oft-posed question: can the humanities be taught?

The two poles of the dilemma, which all who approach the arts must face, are evident in the terms traditionally used to describe or denominate an artwork, whether by past or contemporary theorists. The lexicon is not difficult to assemble, and embraces Aristotle's hylomorphic synolon, as resurrected by the Chicago school; Hegel's concrete universal, the point of departure for some enlightening observations by both John Crowe Ransom and W. K. Wimsatt; "the *universal* which is potentially in each *particular,*" a phrase from Coleridge which has some kinship with Blackmur; and finally one might mention Maritain's "intellectualized sensation," and Father William Lynch's definite-infinite. This far from exhausts the catalogue, but it does point up the bifurcation which any perceptive critic usually makes. In the language of this dualist tradition, which has fairly well dominated our conception of the artwork up to the present, it may be said that the concrete, the singular, is peculiarly, though not exclusively, in the realm of the senses, of the physical—for Aristotle, matter is the principle of individuation; whereas, the universal, the general, is largely the domain of the understanding, of the rational. A poetic work, then, is regarded as a kind of hybrid, partaking of the universal vision of philosophy, and of the pragma of history. The common figure used here in illustration is that of the reasoning animal: the artwork constitutes his typical expression. And since nothing is conceivably more paradoxical than a reasoning animal, the proper structure of poetry will express (with Cleanth Brooks) this paradox, or (with Allen Tate) the tension between all the analogues of this polarity.

43

Almost invariably anyone discussing a work of art tends to accent one or the other of these aspects, whether he be a Chicago neo-Aristotelian (for the middle way is difficult of pursuit, even on the Midway), or one of those critics whose methodological drift has been dated by the adjective "new." The esthete, who corresponds to the earlier impressionist critic, reacts to the richly physical, to what is pejoratively described as the "embellishments." In Gibbon's language, which is here not entirely accurate, such a critic utters the "general encomium, the idle exclamation." The other discussant, who might be called the anesthete, puts, as it were the body of the artifact to sleep so that he may clinically operate upon its soul, its plot. Gibbon's term is in this instance more apposite, for such a critic shows "the exact anatomy" of the object, and sets forth what he believes is its disembodied essence. Both of these unitary views reduce the equilibrium of the art work to a monolithic fragment; they destroy that balanced tension which is the definition of every humanistic discipline, and in seeking to make poetry teachable, they only succeed in making it philosophy or rhetoric. Poetry, *qua* poetry, to be teachable must be taut.

Thus, if the artwork is a synolon, even as man is a synolistic unit, neither exponent of these approaches can be rightly characterized as a humanist: one might be called a sensist, the other a rationalist. We can update these descriptions by employing the epithets that the Chicago school has so vigorously launched: the critic who is concerned with diction primarily, who regards poetry as somehow employing a special language, and who regards this language as its prime constituent, is, in the words of R. S. Crane, a "materialistic monist."[3] Professor Crane who was here attacking Professor Brooks is, of course, snared by his own paradox in suggesting that preoccupation with subject *matter* is spiritual. But Crane's expression is particularly revealing because it implies that an interest in plot is somehow more "spiritual" than an interest in diction; indeed, in most of the theorizing of the neo-Aristotelians there seems to be only a passing awareness of the gnostic dangers in what might just as well be called, "spiritualistic monism."

I do not think, then, that the line of thought which is being developed here, though it stresses by inference the importance of the composite over the segment, will culminate in any accolade to the Chicago critics who have been actively lobbying for the claims of Aristotle as the creator of a genuinely synolistic poetic theory. Phrases like "concrete artistic whole," "structured poetic wholes," abound in the Chicago declarations, and there has been in their denunciations of Messrs Brooks, Ransom, and Empson, a prevalent more-holistic-than-thou attitude. But the totality which the neo-Aristotelians are exalting is analogous to the "wholeness" of the Aristotelian conception of man; whereas, it may be suggested that this is still a fractured wholeness, for there will be a divergence between a poetic which parallels man as a reasoning animal, and a "depth-poetic" which envisions man in his organically existential state: for, as Newman has said, "Man is not a reasoning animal; he is a seeing, feeling, contemplating, acting animal."[4]

Historically speaking, it is not always easy to know just how seriously one is to take Aristotelian principles: the Aristotelians of the neo-classical period were scorned by such later neo-Aristotelians as Butcher, Lane Cooper, and Murray; and the neo-Aristotelians of the Chicago school, which seems rather intent on devouring all its parents—*sicut neo rugiens*—have, in turn, repudiated those precursors. These evolutions and revolutions, these almost marxist re-revisions, are perhaps understandable, for after all, a principle is only a beginning: but one does feel there should be some continuity between the beginning, the middle, and the end, between, say Scaliger, Butcher, and Crane. It may, on the one hand, express a kind of sophisticated theoretical latitudinarianism for Chicago critics to declare that what they are expounding "may not, indeed, except in a general way, be Aristotle at all";[5] but it does not quite diminish in the practical order the narrowness of their dogmatic reliance on their philosopher.

This scholion on the Chicago school and the citation of Gibbon earlier indicate that in the conflict between the advocates of "plot" as the ruling element of a poem, and the proponents of diction, one should opt for the latter. In the manner of the neo-Aristotelians who recurrently seem to remove with the left hand of their dialectic what the right hand has proffered, I would say that in a sense one should, and in a sense one shouldn't. For a dramatic poem, which is all that Aristotle talked about, plot is a dominant factor; for a lyric, it is the structuring of those elements that may be loosely comprised in the term "diction." Aristotle left an outline of something which is "more philosophical," that is, more universal, than history. In such a theory one is presented with the principles for making an object in which a general theme receives only enough physical embodiment to translate it to the auditor or the observer: hence the Aristotelian axiom that "the diction should be elaborated in the pauses of the action," and the low place that "the embellishments of language" hold in the Chicago scheme.

Poetic imitation gives us pleasure because, says the schoolmaster, by it we learn something; in the type of poetry Aristotle is treating of, what we learn or what we contemplate is the concrete universal, with the emphasis on "universal." Aristotle left no theory of the lyric, in which what one has is precisely the converse of what he was discussing: an individual, physical, one might almost say, biological, utterance is given that minimum of "paraphrasable" content which will make it comprehensible to the auditor. Attention is focussed not upon the plot, but upon the emotive force of the poem and the manner in which this force organizes the various other elements that constitute the complete verbal configuration. And the purpose of unifying these purely material, biological utterances is to convey to the listener or reader how powerful is the logos, the word of spirit which can interpenetrate and unify such chaotic, refractory material.

With a nice disregard for the pluralistic finesse of Professor Richard McKeon's postulates, and with a monistic bias as slanted as that which he attributes to Empson or Brooks, and, it may be added, out of what seems a dogged fidelity to the letter of the *Poetics*, Professor Elder Olson succeeds in reducing the lyric to the dramatic; in this reduction, both become subdivisions of the "mimetic" poem:[6]

> Four kinds of action or behavior can thus be distinguished, without regard to seriousness or comicality, etc.: (1) a "closed situation" I mean here one in which the character's activity, *however it may have been initiated or however it may be terminated,* is *uncomplicated* by any other agency. Most of what we call lyric poetry belongs here: any poem in which the character commits some verbal act (threatening, persuading, beseeching) upon someone existing only as the object of his action (Marvell's "To His Coy Mistress"), or deliberates or muses (Keat's "Ode to a Nightingale") or is moved by passion (Landor's "Mother, I Cannot Mind My Wheel").
>
> • • • •
>
> *These are whole and complete "actions";* ...
> [I have supplied the italics for the two clauses.]

47

This passage is from an essay entitled, "An Outline of Poetic Theory," which is drawn up as a philosophical discourse. One regrets that its metaphysical vigor is considerably enervated by such devices as using the word "action" equivocally, with nothing more to justify the attendant ambiguity than quotation marks. It would be rash to attempt to match one's Aristotelian credentials with those of Mr. Olson so I will not question his apparent equation of "action" with "behavior," or his assumption that "action" does not signify as one might have thought it did for Aristotle, the resolution through cause to effect of some operation, but means instead what we would call a "deed." This isolated "deed," this bit of activity, then, corresponds to the plot of the tragedy, and is the "principal part" of the lyric. No one denies that some lyrics possess an argument; certainly Mr. Olson's examples, hardly chosen at random, do. But what about the scores of short poems that do not present "whole and complete 'actions'"? By this critical canon, they are simply blown to gas; and it would seem that on principle they are to be plucked from the anthologies. Aristotle's definition of tragedy included the notes that it is "an imitation of an action that is serious, complete, and of a certain magnitude." The only difference between Aristotle's tragedy and Olson's lyric—"without regard to seriousness or comicality"—would be in their differing "magnitudes": a word that for Aristotle (VII, 4-6) is largely related to size. If one is regarding a "serious" lyric, the major difference between it and, let us say, *King Lear* will be that the former is considerably shorter. It would be difficult even for a "materialistic monist" to accept the conclusion that length constitutes an adequate differentia.

There is a peculiar ambiguity about this paragraph of Professor Olson. We are told that "the character's activity, however it may have been initiated or however it may be terminated".... constitutes a "whole and complete" action. But what has happened to Aristotle's plot which had beginning, middle, and end? We seem to have it and not to have it. That "magnitude" seems to be the major difference between lyric and drama is borne out by the rest of Olson's statement: "These are whole and complete 'actions': hence the first differs from a speech in a play, the second from a dramatic scene, the third from a fragment of a tragedy; nevertheless, it is clear that, *in a sense,* the combination of speeches produces a scene, that of scenes an episode, that of episodes a plot." The ambiguity here is either tendentious or simpliste. If these are whole and complete actions, and the drama is also a whole and complete action, why employ the connective "hence," and follow it by "the first *differs* from a speech in a play..."? An adversative was required here since statedly they differ. But in fact does Professor Olson believe they differ? He does and he doesn't, and hence the inflated amphiboly to disguise as affirmation of belief what is apparently doubt or confusion: "It is clear that, *in a sense,* the combination of speeches produces a scene... of episodes a plot." But a thing is clear or it is not clear; if it is clear *in a sense,* it remains quite obscure. This chiaroscuro maze is further muddled by a later observation that "a lyric does not have plot, but plot is, in fact, the principal part of tragedy." [7] Again, the rhetoric bears examination. The inserted, "in fact," is in a clause which by this time in the essay expresses an unexceptionable Aristotelian truism, so that its being so stressed here can only serve to divert the attention from what is, in fact, the revolutionary principle of the preceding clause, and to reduce it to a kind of *en passant* parenthetic utterance.

Now, as I understand the Aristotelians, poetry is a

form of hazy logic: the beginning, middle, and end of the drama corresponding to the premise, the middle term, and the conclusion of the syllogism. The question then arises how does the lyric which proffers "a whole and complete" action, and yet "does not have plot," give rise to the drama which does? One cannot multiply zeros by zero and come out with a digit—unless it is a *digitus dei ex machina*.

We have, then, not yet resolved the problems of the lyric v. the drama, nor succeeded in subsuming the one in the other. John Crowe Ransom was right when he questioned the ability of even so skilled a thaumaturgist as Kenneth Burke to dramaticize the lyric. Like Olson, though with considerably more range, Burke chose poems with a view to the hurdles to be vaulted, and transformed the rational soul of Aristotle's logical treatises into the intellectual *quodammodo omnia* of the *De Anima*. The neo-Aristotelians of another generation can adjudicate the controversy as to whether this transformation is valid— one would like to think that it is—but it is evident that the current guardians of the text do not approve of these seeming liberties.

Thus Elizabeth Schneider in *Coleridge, Opium, and Kubla Khan,*[1] writes: "My own presupposition.... is that all levels of meaning that may be present in a poem must harmonize with one another and with the emotional tone of the poem as a whole. They must provide a contrapuntal structure in which each theme lends something to each other; they must not together produce a meaningless cacophony. On that presupposition Mr. Warren, Mr. Burke, Mr. Knight, Miss Bodkin, and the others cannot all be right." It is dangerous these days to approach much of anything with presuppositions; it is lethal on their basis to tailor the artifact to one's own pattern, as Miss Schneider does when reading out of the poem lines 29-33.[9] But the important question is why cannot Warren, Knight, et al., be right. Why cannot, as T. S. Eliot has suggested, the poem mean anything you think it means?

The problem is similar to that of a diversity of philosophical systems each of which opposes the other in part and each of which claims to have cornered the truth. I don't know whether it is tenable metaphysics or just a pluralist accommodation to suggest, as have even some Aristotelians—most of them latterly disfranchised—that given the absolute infinite reality all human frameworks of it are at best approximations with only more or less validity. But it is a commonplace among all philosophers to assert that most such systems are generally valid in what they affirm, and defective in what they deny. Not so among the critics, for what could be more affirmative than the readings of that diverse body of critics Miss Schneider has chastised.

But to affirm that "all levels of meaning . . . must harmonize with one another and with the emotional tone of the poem as a whole" is only to beg the question. The issue is to determine the principle of this "harmony." This means we must have a superior element which gives orders to the inferior elements. On Miss Schneider's "presupposition" in the case of a conflict between "meaning" and "tone," it is meaning which provides the criterion. I would say this is valid for the drama, which is a discursive mode of poetry, but invalid for the lyric, which is the work of *intellectus*, and which therefore must express the *quodammodo omnia* of the logos. In this sense the poem can only "mean" whatever one truly knows it to mean.

The drama is, as I have said, a pseudo-philosophical art form; it is more deeply rooted in the world of predictability than the lyric; its very necessity of having beginning, middle, and end, grounds it more in the world of time: whereas the lyric is frequently without tense, and has a kind of non-temporal presence to it which makes it less congenial to theorists who are seeking fixed essences. Plot which the Aristotelians tell us is prime in tragedy is ancillary in the lyric. What is of first importance in the lyric has been described by Blake in his poem on the genesis of poetry.

> Piping down the valleys wild,
> Piping songs of pleasant glee,
> On a cloud I saw a child,
> And he laughing said to me:
>
> "Pipe a song about a Lamb!"
> So I piped with merry cheer.
> "Piper, pipe that song again;"
> So I piped: he wept to hear.
>
> "Drop thy pipe, thy happy pipe;
> Sing thy songs of happy cheer:"
> So I sung the same again,
> While he wept with joy to hear.
>
> "Piper, sit thee down and write
> In a book that all may read."

. . . .

In the drama, rational plot is over-ruling; it governs as does the soul of man, politically and benignly, being moved by the will, and responding occasionally to the solicitings of the senses. In the lyric, plot is relegated to a lesser condition; it functions, if one may draw the analogy, in a manner similar to that in which, theologians tell us, the human knowledge of Christ operated, that is, apart from, but under the regency of his divinity. This "divine" element in the lyric is the constellating of all aspects of the poem so that they constitute a true cosmos; an ordered multiplicity. The exemplary cause of this cosmos, as of every cosmos, is the logos who is Christ, and it is this that the lyric poet is seeking to communicate. The lyric poet, according to Blake, resides in the world of matter and mud and chaos with other men—"the valleys wild" —and is moved, not by what he sees about him, as is the dramatist, but by the vision in the cloud, by the Platonic laughter in the *aria*. For laughter itself is the speech of innocence when man and nature, subject and object, were one in the garden: [10]

> When the meadows laugh with lively green
> And the grasshopper laughs in the merry scene
> When Mary and Susan and Emily
> With their sweet round mouths sing "Ha, Ha, He!"

Laughter, then, is true metaphor in sound; like music it attempts to express sonically the fusion of the I and the Thou, of the lion and the lamb. The poet can only say in temporal sequence: Elizabeth Barrett you are my moon of poets. The woman *is* the moon. How make this subject and this object truly one sonically? It is by that vocalized fusion of sounds which we call laughter; or its poetic counterpart in the utterance of the Belle Dame who makes "sweet *moan*," and of the "woman *wailing*." Because these represent the merging of polarities—which is the goal of all poetry—as Kipling said, "they are the magic. These are vision. The rest is only poetry." The rest being not laughter or sweet moan or wail or music but all that an art which is condemned to be verbal can attain, and which by contrast to the ideal melody of true union—in that perfect metaphor which is the logos—is the difference between[11]

> What a star sang and careless muses heard:
> Old clothes upon old sticks to scare a bird.

The lyric poet first hears the logos-harmony and then tries to relate it to some reality in the world of fact. This is the point of Owen's pararhymes. As Professor Grierson noted, the second rhyme represents the muting of the first. Dramatically, this gives the verse a tone of suspiration, and the half-rhyme is a kind of decline, of reduction from the first, which in a tragic poet may function as an overtone of exhaustion and frustration. But in the deeper sense, these successive mutings point up the nature of lyric as *under*statement: the over-soul is reduced, is diminished, to conform it to the reality of the world of fact. The simple extra-temporal laughing song of union is complicated by its refraction into the temporal and sequential: the logos-image is bent or slanted to reach the domain of the chaotic fact:[12]

> Leaves
>   Murmuring by myriads in the shimmering trees
> Lives
>   Wakening with wonder in the Pyrenees.

Similarly, in *Apologia Pro Poemate Meo* the triplets represent the activating and temporalizing by diffusion of the initial unified logos-insight:

> Merry it was to laugh there—
>   Where death becomes absurd and life absurder
>   For power was on us as we slashed bones bare
>   Not to feel sickness or remorse of murder.

First comes the pure unified melody of Wallace Stevens' "ultimate Plato," then follows the search in the world of "Aristotelian" fact for some analogue to this aria. This fact, which is pre-eminent in tragedy, may be mistaken for the "plot" of the lyric; but the soul of the lyric, as I have already said, is really a kind of over-soul:[13]

> Only by the form, the pattern,
> Can words of music reach
> The stillness, as a Chinese jar still
> Moves perpetually in its stillness.

From this relevance to the world of pure harmony rather than to the world of actual chaotic fact, comes the lyric's explosive force, its glancing strength, its resistance to rational plotting, and its intensity; an intensity so striking that to earlier critics the lyric was defined simply as the poem of "heightened emotion." More circumspectly —and more confusedly—we now give it the name, "short poem." The classification is flawed. For though the impact of *Lear* or *Oedipus* may be quite overwhelming, it is also quite different from that of the lyric (even as the difference between drama and lyric is more than a difference in length), and this because the drama leaves us in the angular domain of fact, while the lyric gives us a vision of the spheres of concord and order. In the drama the requirements of the subject matter shape all the rest, even to the point where "poetry" may be sacrificed to "truth"— though Shakespeare, particularly in the earlier plays, and to the consternation of neo-Aristotelians of every age, will often do the opposite—whereas in the lyric all elements are subordinate to the form, and this form itself is an attempt to adumbrate the ideal form of the logos.

This hegemony of subject matter, of plot, is even more evident in that art form which is more firmly rooted in actuality than the drama. In the novel, particularly in its nineteenth century naturalistic or realistic phase, the entire work seeks to be shaped by the plot, and so-called esthetic requirements are pruned or merely tolerated—like Aristotle's embellishments of language. But even here critical judgment, which generally maintains touch with the rage for order, would affirm the primacy of, say, James over Zola. And it might probably even defend the superiority of *Anna Karenina* over *Resurrection* or *War and Peace*: for while these latter are well-ordered works they derive their order not from the pure urgency of harmony, but from extrinsic metaphysical or ethical principles. And in fact Tolstoy was seeking in *Anna Karenina* the impossible; he was attempting—as do all stylistic purists, whether impressionist or expressionist, whether Woolf or Joyce—to write a lyric novel, a novel that would be more true to the "Platonic" order than to the "Aristotelian" fact. Hence one can applaud the healthy purgative effect of Leavis and his disciples: in their moralizing way they were keeping the genres clean by asserting in the novel the ruling power of the real over the ideal, of the ethical over the esthetic.

The movement from action to image, from dramatic to lyric was a healthy tendency for poetry in the eighteenth century. The movement from action to image in prose fiction sponsored by Bloomsbury, by the Vorticists, Vertigralists, and other verbal innovators of the twenties, and which resulted in O'Faoláin's laments over the vanishing hero, and the decline of plot was necessarily abortive, and might never have arisen had not all distinctions among the various verbal arts become blurred. The critics had been trying to reduce the lyric to the condition of the narrative drama (lyric as "monodrama") and fiction; the playwrights and novelists, true to the Platonic eros, were trying to transmute their forms into the lyric; while the lyricists were trying to write music. (Finally a kind of negative perfection was reached when some of them decided to say nothing.)

Speaking of the lyric species—it having been determined on the grounds adduced above that it could not be a genus—with reference to Yeats' "Sailing to Byzantium," Professor Olson observes: "It is dramatic in manner—the character speaks in his own person; and the medium is words embellished by rhythm and rhyme."[4] This is the younger Elder Olson writing some years before his examination of the poetry of Dylan Thomas—an examination which was valuable largely because it employed the methodology of the new critics—and so one is inclined to dismiss as the result of too passionate a devotion to his philosopher the rather cavalier assertion that the "medium is words embellished by rhythm and rhyme." This kind of talk would not be surprising in a critic writing nearly half a millennium before this era, but we know a poetry considerably more extensive than the merely dramatic, a poetry in which diction does not function as mere decoration; and this wider extension is apparent in the title of another Chicago statement to which I have referred above, "From Action to Image," by Norman Maclean. We know a poetry, and not a degenerate poetry, nor a poetry indicative of a declension in values, as Maclean would seem to see it, which is predominantly a poetry of the organization of images, of phantasms, a poetry which resides in the "embellishments," and which uses meter and rhythm—to employ the kind of physiological imagery favored by Aristotelians—not simply as the frosting that makes the metaphysical cake palatable, but as constituting the cake itself.

There would seem to be empirically evident a poetry of the ultimately concrete individual thing, a poetry of the fragmented realm of discontinuity, of the discrete, a poetry which is apparently of the senses, of that Aristotelian "matter" which is the principle of individuation and which is defined as "part outside of part," and which is, also by definition, unknowable. It is not the poetry which is more philosophical, because more universal, than history; if anything it is the poetry which is as non-philosophical, as non-universal, and hence as ahistorical as any comprehensible statement can be, and which notwithstanding all those seeming obstacles to comprehension is nevertheless significant, is nevertheless, as all experience attests, more significant than the drama. This greater significance—though logically undemonstrable—can derive in the lyric only from the one source of all meaning in the universe: from the lyric's deeper participation in the life of the logos of the spirit. This is why the lyric which seems, by contrast to the drama, so formless, so chaotic, so fragmented, nevertheless has so great an impact on man.

We are faced here with a datum of experience: we respond with greater ardor to the apparent disorder of the lyric than to the provable order of the drama. There can be but one reason: that the lyric speaks to us on a higher level than that of our rational faculty; but there is *no* higher level than that of *intellectus*, logos, spirit.

The dramatic poetry Aristotle envisioned was a poetry which raised the individual event to universal import; history was simply the concatenation of individual deeds; while above these two lower orders was the domain of the essential, of the universal. But might not one posit another lyric level, even less "philosophical" than history which, after all, does admit of some universalization, that is, the level of the supremely unique, the level of things in which we rejoice not because they tell us more about ourselves, nor because we have something immediately in common with them, but in which we seem to find delight precisely because they are so different from ourselves and so different from one another. It is the level on which we encounter, among other things,[15]

> All things counter, original, spare, strange:
> Whatever is fickle, freckled (who knows how?) ...

It is the level which gives us paradoxically by reason of its very concreteness the best vision of the infinite spirit-world of harmony: for, as St. Thomas says "similitudes drawn from things farthest away from God form within us a truer estimate that God is above whatsoever we may think or say." (I, I. 9 ad. 3) This is to make a link between poetry and prayer which recent criticism has tended to discredit: yet empirically speaking the only reason history proffers for modern thinkers from Arnold to Cassirer regarding poetry as a substitute religion is precisely because that *is what it is.*

To say that what I refer to is a poetry of the sense, of the phantasm, of the principle of utter individuation, is not to say that it is somehow a-human or infra-human. With the Greek Fathers, it is to suggest that even as at the incarnation of the Word not only was spirit materialized, but in a sense, matter was spiritualized, so, too, this poetry is all the more truly human simply because its rich physicality is nevertheless spiritual. It is all the more meaningful because it seems patently so meaningless. Aristotle might have regarded such poetry as disordered in character, even as a contemporary philosopher, Max Picard, following Aristotle's doctrine on marriage has described the sexual union as on the plane of discontinuity, as a kind of rupture of the higher plane of being, as, in fact, an abdication of reason. However, man's entrance into the order of humanized matter need not entail an intellectual abdication, but may be an intentional act, a conscious and deliberate submission to his deeper non-rational spirituality, and hence a fully human act. I think a re-appraisal of Aristotle along these lines might provide the basis for illustrating that type of lyric which is not description, not explanation, but the articulation of that which reaches beyond the limits of its apparent motive—passion for the undefined.

Since I am talking about passion, about, in the best sense of the word, sensation, about the uniquely individual, I am necessarily talking about the principle in which passion, sensation, individuality, are rooted, that is, about matter. I return, then, to the "utterance of matter," to that which expresses this supreme individuality. In critical terms I return to the image and the phantasm, and to those other factors which make up the language of the discrete. But it is necessary to emphasize that strictly or loosely speaking, matter alone cannot "utter" itself; cannot "ex-press" its supreme individuality unless informed by spirit, by logos. It is this tension between the "absolutely" spiritual and the "absolutely" physical (a tension which only God can sustain and towards which the poet can only aspire) in the lyric which makes it so impatient of analysis; for analysis by definition requires not tension but slackness or limpness.

I should add parenthetically that I am refraining from setting forth any axiological judgments here: there may be a poetry of which "plot is the soul" and of which image, rhythm, and meter constitute merely superficial decoration: the drama would seem to exemplify it. There is historically apparent a poetry which is virtually plotless, in which plot is tertiary and of which such disparate elements as image, rhythm, and meter are the accidents revealing the essence: logos. This is not necessarily to express any preference for one type or the other; it is simply to affirm that both exist.

However, even non-Aristotelians have subscribed to the assumption that all poetry is essentially dramatic. Thus Wimsatt and Beardsley: "But even a short lyric poem is dramatic, the response of a speaker (no matter how abstractly conceived) to a situation (no matter how universalized)."[16] But in these terms every expression is "dramatic," (and by the same token, "lyric") and the word becomes so generalized in its application as to be diluted of all real content. Cleanth Brooks has also noted that "the structure of a poem resembles that of a play,"[17] but he does little to clarify the assertion, for which failure he was duly taken to task by Professor Crane. With neither Wimsatt nor Brooks, however, does the idea of the lyric as a "play" approach the definition of dramatic action of the neo-Aristotelians—though Wimsatt and, more recently, Father William Lynch, seem to incline in that direction. But if there is a dramatic element in much "non-dramatic" lyric poetry, it is by using the term, "drama," in strict analogy, as *simpliciter* different, *secundum quid* the same: the "drama" resides in the relation of verbal and metered constructs, in the sustaining of tensions, and in the resolution of conflicting expressions. The lyric is not a play, but an interplay. It is the interplay of that logos which, as Hopkins well knew "plays in *ten thousand* places," that is, plays in the realm of multiplicity.

Certainly plot is basic to such a pseudo-philosophical art form as tragedy—which perhaps explains why philosophers from Aristotle to the present have talked considerably more about it than about the lyric. One notes that the only two exercises in "practical" criticism in the manual of the Chicago school are on *King Lear* and *Tom Jones*: not exactly lyric pieces. Moreover, when Mr. Olson does provide a new insight or suggest a valuable approach to the poems of Dylan Thomas, he does so largely by escaping from the framework of his own system and relying on the techniques of critics such as Tate or Brooks; in fact, he shows himself as close a reader of the *OED* as Empson —even to the point of providing a lexicon of Thomas' terms.

Beyond their extraordinary historical scholarship, which is very broad—as befits men caught up in the temporal— one has the impression that it is mainly by ignoring a good deal of extant literature, or by re-reading it from a fixed, pre-determined viewpoint, or finally, by unwittingly slipping into the methodology of the opposition school, and then climactically attributing their successful achievement to Aristotelian principles—it is by these devices that generally speaking the Chicago critics have successfully fielded so many sorities against the poor old new critics. As one would expect of philosophers, the Chicagoans have fired some devastating salvos in general theory: their big guns on the front of practical criticism have usually sent forth light squibs.

I have discussed the first and the third of these devices above; I would like briefly to treat now of the second: the fixed, pre-determined viewpoint which distinguishes their writings. Elder Olson, who is the most astute theorist of this group, in an essay entitled, "William Empson, Contemporary Criticism, and Poetic Diction," declared:[16]

> And the profundity and complexity in poetry which so much interests Empson is due primarily to action and character, which cannot be handled in grammatical terms, rather than to diction, which can. That profundity is only in a small degree verbal, in the sense that verbal analysis will yield the whole of it; and even then it is very seldom a matter of verbal ambiguity. Shakespear's profoundest touches are a case in

point. "Pray you, undo this button" and "The table's full" are profound, not as meaningful verbal expressions but as actions permitting an extraordinary number of implications, in that they are revelatory of many aspects of character and situation.

In this case, Shakespeare's "profoundest touches" are so defined by fiat only. The circularity of the argument is what is here revelatory, and since whatever is freely asserted may be freely denied, one is justified in disproving Olson's contention by simply declaring, what many would take to be a truism, that Shakespeare's profoundest touches are to be found in such exciting linguistic collisions as Ransom has discussed in his study, "On Shakespeare's Language": lines like

> Will all great Neptune's ocean wash this blood
> Clean from my hand? No; this my hand will rather
> The multitudinous seas incarnadine,
> Making the green one red.
>
> ("Macbeth," II, ii, 60-63)

This Shakespearean fusion of Latin and Anglo-saxon functions here, as do all the "embellishments" of diction employed by the lyric genius, as the blending of the two worlds; as the dual vision of the hard material Anglo-saxon fact and the reflected mediated-by-intellect logos-fiction which the poetic mind half creates and half perceives. Such linguistic combinations are the expression of poetry itself, as the attempt to bring together the laughing aria of "Platonic" harmony which the spirit hears, and the harsh "Aristotelian" chaos in which we actually dwell. The weaving serpentine latin polysyllables of the "ultimate Plato" blend with the hard Anglo-saxon gruntings of Aristotle and we encounter the "heavenly labials in a world of gutturals" of Wallace Stevens.

63

Poetry dwells in the twi-lights and mediates between the loud abstracting sunlight and the silence of incomprehensible darkness. Latin and Anglo-saxon are the English poet's unique instrument for expressing this oxymoronic character of all art, its character as neither the definite horizontal nor the infinite vertical, but the diagonal of Coleridge's "chasm which slanted." Its muse is Keats' Belle Dame who "sideways would she lean." The poem weaves like an arabesque between the two poles of day and night, of universal and concrete, of Aristotle pointing down and Plato pointing up, of the definite and the infinite; and like Yeats' with his inter-twining gyres, the poem would like to have the best of both whorls.

The poem is the river which meanders with "a mazy motion," and it is Hulme's "snake's body" with "coils which go contrary ways." Because of its serpentine convolutions it has never been captured alive by the philosophers. The trophies of dead poetry with which the metaphysicians adorn their square cells have nothing to do with the weaving creature of poetic paradox:

> With burnished neck of verdant Gold...
> With tract oblique ... side-long he works his way.
> (*Paradise Lost*, IX, 501, 510)

What the philosophical dissertations give us is at best the mathematical charting of the trajectory of this strange beast; with the result that the poem, which shrinks, as Wallace Stevens says, "from the light of primary noon," is killed by the clear light of the abstractionist's verbal algebra. 'Tis the bright day that brings forth the poisonous philosophical adder—and subtractor and divider as well. And the abstractionist falls from critical grace precisely because he lacks the charism to cover this multitude of sinuosities.

Since I will have no occasion to refer to it later, I would add parenthetically that this oxymoronic vision in which the harmony of Plato is fused with the chaos of Aristotle, accounts in our tradition for rhyme. Three little kittens never lost their mittens, but we are quite willing, for the sake of verbal concord to transcend—while rooted in it— the factual literalness of things. Rhyme, of course, may have a rhetorical-dramatic function as W. K. Wimsatt has shown in one of his most engaging essays, but this function in the lyric poem is accidental. And so too with that clash between an infinite latinity and defined Anglo-saxon in the lyric, which is my present concern.

In Shakespeare such collisions have not primarily a dramatic purpose as they do for example in de La Mare's "Sam"—who is the Old Testament Samuel listening to the voice of another world:

> Wonderful lovely there she sat,
> Singing the night away
> All in the solitudinous sea
> Of that there lonely bay.

The collision between a latinity dignified by Shakespeare's use of it and a vulgar colloquialism in this passage has a "dramatic" purpose: to point up the conflict between the imaginative insight of Sam's childhood and the pragmatic cerebration of his old age. Though here as elsewhere, the collision is derived from the larger figure I have set forth above on poetry as mediating the two worlds of chaos and harmony. Again Anglo-saxon and latinity merge dramatically—though again derivative from the larger figure since all drama derives from lyric—in Sassoon's "Prehistoric Burials."

> These barrows of the century-darkened dead,—
> Memorials of oblivion, these turfed tombs
> Of muttering ancestries whose fires, once red,
> Now burn for me beyond mysterious glooms.

Here we are polarizing the primitive man with his alleged-ly simple animism and modern self-reflecting man with his ratiocinative probings. But that poet whom Sassoon is unknowingly following across Salisbury Plain (*The Prelude*, XIII, 313 ff) though personally straitened by the relation of mediate and immediate vision employs these linguistic collisions for their essentially lyric purpose.

> The ghostly language of the ancient earth
> II, 309
> with a countenance
> Of Adoration with an eye of love
> II, 413
> Redoubled and redoubled, concourse wild
> Of jocund din.
> V, 378

But the point of this excursus has been to suggest a counter-tactic to Elder Olson's assertion that Shakespeare's profoundest touches "are profound, not as meaningful verbal expressions but as actions...." And the *sed contra* above will be equally applicable to any lyric genius.

Indeed, if we accepted Olson's rule of thumb concerning Shakespeare's diction we would have great difficulty in accounting for "Shakespearean style." Richard II does sound at times like Lady Macbeth, who in turn sounds like Lear, who in turn..., and so on through the whole gamut of characters: in fact, they all sound like Shakespeare. This would not be even partially true if their various utterances were all born of strict dramatic exigency and directed only to disclosing the personality of the character and the tendency of his actions.

The first three elements of Aristotle's schema can to a considerable degree be comprehended by reason alone; the fourth, not so, because it is in the order of the spiritually informed, individually unique; it is not merely the product of yoking the steeds of thought to the inert chariot of imagery, it is not merely the product of rational meaning and irrational phantasm, which product may then be critically examined posteriorly by separating the composite; it entails something beyond mere rational analysis, something similar to that judgment of style which, for Longinus "is the last and crowning fruit of long experience." Aristotle has little of relevance to say concerning diction; he seems to group it with song, of which he insouciantly remarks, "it is a term whose sense everyone understands"—everyone, that is, living three hundred years B. C.

The mention of Longinus provides me with a convenient hinge to turn this topic around to the pedagogical issue I mentioned in the beginning. For Longinus' teaching, or what has conventionally been accepted as an important part of that teaching, is cardinal in the development of the present argument which may be put in terms of Allen Tate's question:[19]

Can there be a criticism of convincing objectivity which approaches the literary work through the analysis of style and which arrives at its larger aspects through that aperture?

I am not too sure that "aperture" is the proper word here, since nothing is more manifest than the meter or diction of the work, and to treat either as some kind of obscure and indistinguishable entrance to the poem often engenders that kind of depth-plumbing criticism one sometimes finds in the strained and labored exercises of the *Explicator*. One is tempted to inquire of such critics, as of other journeyman plumbers, whether they had a hard day at the orifice.

But two points in the *Peri Hypsous* are significant here: first, the assertion that an artwork is not sublime, if it exhibits occasionally "invention schooled by experience," or merely a "fine order and distribution of its parts." A sublime poetic expression is not simply an aggregate of stylistic devices as some verbal analysts would have it, nor, on the other hand, is it merely a decorated structure of ideas and themes, as the neo-Aristotelians would seem to regard it. It is not a sub-rational, nor a rational creation, but an object which in its genesis and effect is trans-rational—that is to say, eminently *intellectual;* an object, all the constituents of which are pierced by sublimity (read *spirit*) "as by a flash of lightning." And by all the constituents is meant *all*, including integrally and organically the elements of diction, meter, and imagery. Longinus was not a forerunner of Empson, but if he must be regarded as a precursor of any contemporary critical trend, it will be one which is linguistic rather than thematic.

The second point from the *Peri Hypsous*, which should be emphasized here, is bound up with Longinus' statement that the sublime "affects us not to persuade but to entrance." The word is *ekstasis* which is literally a transport, and it, like the artwork itself, has had a schizoid career, being understood, on the one hand, in an extended though not distorted sense as the expression of Romantic agony, and, on the other hand, as the empathic identification of the audience with the speaker. Since the *Peri Hypsous* is a rhetorical treatise, the second meaning is primary; but since any and all knowledge implies a kind of identification between subject and object, and the particular identification Longinus refers to is accompanied, more or less, by such psycho-physical accompaniments as frenzy, mad enthusiasm, and wild passion, there is good reason to accept the Romantic reading quite literally as ecstasy, and to view the poem as a kind of narcopaedic device for translating us—while leaving us in it—from the "Aristotelian" chaos to the "Platonic" harmony.

But poetry is not an instrument of "escape" in the crude sense of the word. The sinuous chameleon of Keats which through successive avatars passes from "heart aches" through the "drowsy numbness" to "such an ecstasy" is not fleeing reality, but rather using the things of this world as if he used them not, in order to attain the vision of the heavenly Jerusalem of Plato, of the lasting city built on the seven story mount Abora. The poem is the Platonic honeydew which silvers the Aristotelian mud.[20]

> And whence they came and whither they shall go
> The dew upon their feet shall manifest.

In the "solution sweet" of Longinian ekstasis we are moved into the perichoretic harmony where by metaphor Apollo *is* thrice-great Hermes, where truth *is* beauty, where subject *is* object, where alpha *is* omega: a harmony which can be imaged out in the oxymoronic circle, in the Grecian urn, in the sunny dome of ice, in the jar in Tennessee that makes the wilderness "no longer wild," in the silent horn of Eben Flood, in the egg of Gide and the "cold sphere" of Mann. The poem is the rite of circularity and "Ceremony's a name for the rich horn."[21]

The biography of this term, ecstasy, reflects the same

**69**

dualism encountered earlier. The first meaning of *ekstasis* (beyond its rhetorical reference) stresses our sympathetic identification with the speaker in a rational bond which, though affecting the senses and intellect, remains basically a thing of the reason; the second meaning emphasizes the physical and biological concomitants which accompany any truly incarnational experience. In Maclean's terms, the first may be related primarily to the poetry of action, the second to the poetry of image; the one primarily to the drama, the other to the lyric.

I have no quarrel with the advocates of the first emphasis, nor with the pre-eminent position they assign to dramatic action in tragedy. I suggest again, however, that this informing function of the rational plot whereby it is conceived as the soul, not only of tragedy, but of all poetry, simply does not hold for much lyric work. As I have said, if dramatic poetry is similar to the notion of man as a reasoning animal with a fixed, constant structure, then lyric poetry is analogous to the idea of man, certainly not as irrational, but as possessing a kind of utterly free spiritual daimonic character. This is not an either-or proposition; one can accent, as one wishes, any aspect of the multifold complexity which is man. But if one does not want to negate the important service Aristotelian critics have done in the field of drama, neither can the fact be overlooked that in the equally arable field of the lyric, they have squinted at the poetic object as if to deliquesce its materiality, and refine or vaporize its richly physical contours —all with the apparent hope that this critical distillation will emerge from their rational alembic as some kind of pure gnostic reality. They are like those philosophical people who are forever lauding grace of soul, "spiritual" beauty, etc. Though in truth[22]

It might well be that their mistress
Is no gaunt fugitive phantom.
She might, after all, be a wanton,
Abundantly beautiful, eager,

Fecund,
From whose being by starlight, on sea-coast
The innermost good of their seeking
Might come in the simplest of speech.

I would like, then, to center this part of the discussion
on those elements in the poetic object which transcend
rational analysis, and yet which do form an essential part
of the poem. Perhaps with the statement that I am concerned about the non-rational it will seem that this essay
is to be read as a defense of the extremest romanticism.
Perhaps this is true; yet I think the presence of a non-
rational or trans-rational element in the artwork to be as
scientifically verifiable as that there is a trait in man, specifically human (no brute is daimonic, and, for that matter,
neither is any demon), and nevertheless beyond the direct
control or grasp of reason.

But one might contend at this point that if one is
concerned with what is not rational, then, all possibility of
communication has been interdicted, for there can be no
dialogue on a non-rational topic between rational beings.
Perhaps it has been the recognition of this impossibility
which has unconsciously led various neo-Aristotelians and
crypto-Cartesians to over-emphasize the role of plot or
argument: that *is* something one can talk about, and since
it seems to be the function of critics to talk, they under-
standably tend to ignore or to relegate to an inferior order
whatever is (from their point of view) unspeakable or
(from my point of view) ineffable. But before discussing
the possibility of communicating the non-rational, I would

71

like briefly to point out another peril in any emphatically rationalist approach to the artwork.

Such an emphasis tends to substitute, on the part of the auditor or reader or viewer, a discursive analytic attack upon the object for its synoptic contemplative comprehension. It tends therefore—and in this lies the inadequacy of the Chicago program—to make criticism the instrument for grasping the poem, and hence ultimately to exalt it above the esthetic and ecstatic experience itself. This is borne out in an otherwise innocuous statement of Professor Crane: "... criticism as distinct from *mere* aesthetic perception or appreciation, is reasoned discourse...."[23] Nothing more strikingly underlines the despotic rationalism of the Chicago school than this pronouncement: for, in this *mere* are submerged all those pious protestations of loyalty to the art object which have emanated from the Midway. One imagines that students at Chicago might reply as did the Cambridge girl when Robert Graves asked her what poems she most enjoyed; huffily answering, in the best ruthless talk of the undergraduate, she noted that "Poems are not meant to be enjoyed, but to be analyzed."

A similar rationalism is to be encountered in most textbooks of appreciating or "understanding" poetry. Thus a recent manual, after outlining various analytic techniques which "should be only the preparation for our own experience and enjoyment of the work," continues:[24]

In the actual experience of a work of art, all the points of which we have spoken are blended together into a unified whole. We are able to achieve this only when we have developed *good taste*. For a person of good taste the process of analysis of which we have been speaking becomes second nature, so that there is no need to think of it; only the beauty of the work is present. There is little use in learning rules of literary criticism unless we use them so frequently that they become second nature. Reference to them, however, will be useful in approaching new and unfamiliar types of works, and in discussing works with friends.

Good taste, then consists in a facility in focussing the rules of analysis upon the artifact, so that what the novice critic does laboriously the man of taste does with ease; and the way to acquire this "taste" is to use over and over again the "rules of literary criticism." But this is to put the part before the source. All that analysis can reach are the disjointed elements of the work; it cannot bring about the personal encounter with the being of the poem, with that unique configuring force that constitutes the poemness of the work—and which happens to be what we are after.

The dominant heresy of Aristotelian critics is not what Cleanth Brooks has called the "heresy of paraphrase," it is what theologians call "traditionalism" or "fideism." The traditionalists taught that man could not by his own power come to the knowledge of any absolute truth, that is, to the knowledge of spirit which is the ground of all absolutes. They therefore posited some primitive revelation which had been handed down through the generations and which accounted for present-day man's knowledge of the existence of God, of providence, etc. Something similar to this is responsible for the notion that we can come to an appreciation of a particular poem by determining the degree to which it conforms to "the rules of art." The question necessarily arises how do we determine the right rules of art. The only answer is that we deduce them from existing works of avowedly great art. From an examination of all the masterpieces ever created we can condense a thousand rules, or a hundred, or ten—depending on the pedagogical level we are on. But the next question arises:

73

how did we determine which were the masterpieces from which to condense our rules? Ultimately we are driven to conclude either that there was a primitive revelation of the first masterpiece, from which the first rules were deduced, or that the first man—and presumably his successors —possessed an innate capacity for recognizing the truly beautiful. In the light of the second alternative, the first is absurd, and must be abandoned; and the task for the pedagogue remains to bring his charges into the same situation and disposition as that first man encountering that first beautiful object. If it was good enough for Adam it ought to be good enough for us.

The paragraph I have quoted above represents the type of doxy to which educators are prone to succumb. They need a convenient technique, readily teachable, and capable of measurable results. The jibing of a poem with some pre-ordained canon, and the deduction of excellence from the degree of enmeshment, offers just such an instrument. One regrets, while understanding, that teaching so readily inclines to materialization; for what these methodists have in fact given us is the esthetic counterpart of that myth of biological man which is reflected in books bearing such titles as "How to Develop Personality," "How to Fall in Love," etc. The truth is that these materialists mistrust intellect and feel at home only in the realm of reason: they never feel warm unless the thermometer certifies the experience.[25]

> He sets this peddler's pie and cries in summer.
> The glass man, cold and numbered, dewily cries,
> "Thou art not August unless I make thee so."

Furthermore, it is evident that anyone who is effectively engaged in the teaching of literature—the author of the

quoted paragraph above is a "professional" philosopher—
realizes the inadequacy of discursive analytic techniques
in comprehending the artifact.[26] Thus Stanley Hyman has
observed of the eight years of teaching literature that inter-
vened between the first and second editions of *The Armed
Vision:* "As the principal change in my views, I would
now incline to see the act of evaluation not as a super-
structure erected upon analysis, but as an informal pro-
cedure antecedent to analysis, in determining whether any
given work warrants the expenditure of that much critical
labor."

The methodists are right in rooting the esthetic experience in a conjunction; but what is conjoined is not the
poem and the "rules of literary criticism," but the incarnate logos of the poem and the incarnate logos of the
reader. The poem is the concrete universal, the product
of intellectualized sensation, and therefore like man, exists
in paradox. And hence as Cleanth Brooks has stressed, the
language of poetry is the language of paradox. But the
language of man in fact, is rarely the language of paradox, since man, immersed in the world of doing and making, in the world of neg-otium, in the world which destroys
the otium sanctum, must in order to survive, speak the
palaver of action or the cant of reason: that is, he must
orient himself to one or the other pole of his nature. He
will tend to commute back and forth between the gen-
eralities of reason's *ex*tension and the fragments of sensation's *in*tention; he will rarely exist—to employ the critical
algebra of Allen Tate—in that perfect tension, which, like
virtue, is radicated in the middle. But man seeks to free
himself (*licere*-leisure) from the world of busy-ness, and
to rest in the world of being: in Kierkegaard's terms he
seeks to become what he is; that is, he seeks to perfect, to
exercise his unique is-ness and to relate it to the is-ness

75

about him in that "drawing out" process which defines education and ecstasy, and which takes place in the school.

When Yeats in "Prayer for My Daughter," asks that she may have "natural kindness," he is praying simply that she will become what she is: "to become what she is," is pleonasm, as is the expression "natural *kind*ness." Yeats then intensifies the paradox by praying that all "her business" will "be in dispensing round": her business will be in pensée which is "round": her action will be in contemplation, which as the Scholastics knew, is circular; her doing in being. She will exist in that balanced tension which defines both man and the poem.

In the early stages of education when the child is yet immersed in intractable matter and his hold on his own unique being is slight, he must be presented with artifacts to which he can be related, whether they are crude narrative poetry or popular music. The only virtue to be instilled in this period is absolute self-honesty, so that no social or environmental pressures interfere with his instinct for contemplative rest, so that nothing inhibits his desire to progress to a balanced artifact, to travel further in Keats' "realms of gold." In every stage of his progress, of his education of being, he will encounter a work of art which though unbalanced, though fundamentally sensual, has sufficient being about it to move him (however the scale of his advance may be graduated) to reach out to that artifact which is not deficient, which is not ugly—the privation of being constituting ugliness. When his being is so fully matured, when he has become what he is, then in the order of beauty, which is the only transcendental we are concerned with here, he has taste. The being which he is encounters the being in the artifact; if he cannot rest in this union, or if his being cannot "meet" the deficient being of a particular work, he then knows this to be an inferior or ugly or defective work. He knows this non-rationally and non-discursively in an immediate juncture or disjuncture of being.

Someone may question the evaluation of the man of taste, may doubt that he really knows whether a particular work is "beautiful." To those who do not see what he sees, he can only reply with Newman, "I know I am right. How do you know it? I know I know. How? I know I know I know etc. etc." [27] The kind of assessment resulting from this existential union admits of that high degree of refinement which explains the extreme precision of certain judgments of Bernard Berenson or the almost micrometric exactitude of the following *non sequitur* from Mr. Eliot: "Dante is as great as Milton and at least as great as Shakespeare." [28]

If we must assign some social end to the arts, this would be the place to do it: they put man in his proper metaphysical stance, they perfect him as person. With this truly "educative" basis we are preserved against the Aristotelian "inducative" biological analogy which reduces the reader to Cummings' "Mr. Vinal":

> ... (who tensetendoned and with
> upward vacant eyes, painfully....

and which reduces the poem to "food for the mind," as in Milton's shockingly vulgar reference (*Paradise Lost*, VII, 126-30). And on the other hand we are saved from the temptation of subordinating the arts to some didactic end. Because we recognize that the poem should have a palpable design—"as old medallions to the thumb," says the meaningful poem—we recognize, too, that we should fear, as Keats said, "poetry that has a palpable design upon us."

In the natural order the poem provides the supremely

contemplatable object. It takes us through chaos into order, and hence the poet is traditionally the transforming sorcerer, the mountebank, the conjuror whose charm is carmen and whose grammar is glamour. But the sense of this sleight of hand man, as Stevens punned it, is precisely that: slight. He employs not the large gestures and the overstatement of the man of action, nor the silent immobility of the mystic, but the understatement which makes us do nothing: [29]

> it survives
> In the valley of its saying where executives
> Would never want to tamper.

The poem, because it suspends us at the mid-point between the poles of the paradox which constitutes man and his typical expression, has nothing to say to morality or to pragma on any level. That poem which sets us in motion, which destroys this polar tension by inducing in the man of taste some pious or patriotic or prurient experience, is by that fact defective: it is not overheard, but heard. And this defect may mar that work which is ethical as well as that which is pornographic. Obviously, I am not now talking of the artist's intention, which is irrelevant provided his execution is not flawed, but about the experience of the auditor or viewer.

There is, of course, a relation between poetry and morality, or, better, between poetry and the deepest roots of religion, but this relationship is not to be found in any Aristotelian notion that poetry gives us a heightened perception of history, that it provides us with concrete instances of man's nature, motives, etc. I think this relationship is, as usual in the arts, something negative, and may be described as follows. The reader of a poem, as in all human activity, has some awareness of self, of his own human consciousness, when contemplating the object. He is implicitly aware of himself as the subject of whatever emotional-intellectual response his grasp of the artifact may elicit. When this response reaches its maximum intensity the reader is recalled from a consideration of the poem to a consideration of what is taking place within his own consciousness. He experiences an illumination of his own being. From this contemplation of the art-object, so great an awareness of his own existential state is engendered that he undergoes an intuition of his own contingency, and immediately the flame of his being aspires to the light which burns unconsumed. The absolute and the contingent reach towards each other:[30]

> Ramon Fernandez, tell me, if you know,
> Why, when the singing ended and we turned
> Toward the town, tell why the glassy lights,
> The lights in the fishing boats at anchor there,
> As the night descended, tilting in the air,
> Mastered the night and portioned out the sea,
> Fixing emblazoned zones and fiery poles,
> Arranging, deepening, enchanting night

Ramon Fernandez—the rationalist, the moralist debating Rivière—cannot tell us: there is no question mark because there is in fact no question.

The various methodists of criticism seem to regret that the artifact does not represent a clear, reasonable thing; and perhaps from the professional viewpoint of a critic (a "professional critic" being like a "professional saint" or a "professional lover of wisdom") it is regrettable. They seem rather uncomfortable with the assumption, which to many is a fact almost clinically certified, that the poem resides in the world of mystery, not in that of problem.

Nor is this to speak figuratively: the definition of mystery in Marcel's terminology is a union of subject and object: thus the ultimate mystery of an infinite being, God, is defined as the *coincidentia oppositorum*, as the circumincession of alpha and omega. And every lesser mystery can be approached only by that same path, by the *via invia* of language which we call metaphor: for metaphor is, like the contemplation of the artifact itself, a union of subject and object through the bond of being.[31]

> And these black bodies and this sun-burnt face
> *Is* but a cloud.

Problem which is rooted in action, in doing and making, keeps subject and object separate, or acknowledges through simile, the gap between them.[32]

> Many sisters and brothers
> Like birds in their nest
> Are ready for rest.

The poet by his simile declares that he knows the two elements are not one, though he will treat them "as if" they were. This "as if" represents the invasion of reason, of that self-reflection which turns the mind back upon its own operations and prohibits it from going out and embracing the object. This is borne out by the preceding stanzas of this same poem of Blake: the only simile in the poem is in this third stanza, the stanza of darkness, of the domain of experience, of the "divided image." Here men and nature are no longer one as they were in the metaphors of the day stanzas. Here unifying love becomes divisive lust, intellect becomes reason. The subject is not one with the object: the subject *does* something to the object: from the lyric of being we move to the drama of action.

Blake's simile is entirely functional: it hints at the inevitable fall from the single vision of innocence to the split vision of experience. Metaphor says union, simile says union mediated by reason, that is unreal union. It is the difference between poetry and prose, between mystery and problem, between imagination and reason, for, in Keats' famous statement, "the imagination may be compared to Adam's dream—he awoke and found it truth."

This evolution from metaphor to simile, from fruitful union-with-the-object-in-mystery to sterile relation-with-the-object-in-problem is brought out more emphatically by Blake in the first Holy Thursday poem, of which I am quoting the complete text:

'Twas on a Holy Thursday, their innocent faces clean,
The children walking two and two, in red and blue and green,
Grey-headed beadles walked before, with wands as white as snow,
Till into the high dome of Paul's they like Thames' waters flow.

O what a multitude they seemed, these flowers of London town!
Seated in companies they sit with radiance all their own.
The hum of multitudes was there, but multitudes of lambs,
Thousands of little boys and girls raising their innocent hands.

Now like a mighty wind they raise to Heaven the voice of song,
Or like harmonious thunderings the seats of Heaven among.
Beneath them sit the aged men, wise guardians of the poor;
Then cherish pity, lest you drive an angel from your door.

Childhood is innocence and animism and union of imagination; it constructs the metaphor which is true; age is experience and religiosity (religion in Blake being a pejorative: St. Paul's being not the tabernacle of God, but the temple of Urizen, of theology) and the abstractions of

81

reason. In these lines the children's metaphors are contrasted with the similes of the aged. Mystery is contrasted with problem: beadles with wands white *as* snow: "they" (the antecedent is "beadles") flow *like* the Thames; but children *are* flowers; children *are* lambs. The last stanza with its dominating similes, and by the stylistic reversal in which the figures precede the subjects, represents the swallowing up of innocence by experience, of mystery by problem, of metaphor by simile. The hortative conclusion—prose rhetoric being the only way of communicating with adults—means in the world of Aristotelian fact: "be kind to the poor children." But in the Platonic vision of Blake and of every other poet, the admonition is to remember the innocence from which we came. We are the angels; we transcend discursive reason and are united in true metaphor only when we return to our past. Pity is the natural piety which makes us reverence that childhood which was father to this manhood, that childhood of true religion when as Nature's Priest, by metaphor we re-united what as adults we see as separated. And Blake rightly insists that mystery and metaphor are not just refinements or higher degrees of problem and simile, but an entirely different domain: the domain of the logos where we meet the God of Abraham, Isaac, and Jacob, not the God of philosophers.

This distinction between problem and mystery is probably too bad for critics, though it is certainly good for the poets, who after all are not among us merely in order that what they mutter may provide fodder for "reasoned discourse," and who do enjoy something more than simply temporal priority or causal eminence. The neo-Aristotelian critics bring to mind certain of their medieval predecessors who, in theology, after defining God as the all-mysterious, incomprehensible, inscrutable, supreme Being, then proceeded to systematically analyze the object of their thought with such surgical nicety as to belie all their apophatic premises: the only difference between the two types of rationalist being that the theologian at least once had to acknowledge the presence of mystery. True, it is a better thing *for rational discourse* if the deity be rationalized, but one may then find oneself treating not of what *is*, but of some manufactured surrogate. Rational discourse is not the only attainment of the mind, nor, as I hope to indicate later, its best mode of communication. Newman's statement on "Romantist theology" cuts both ways.[33]

> It may be said to leave no region unexplored, no heights unattempted, rounding off its doctrines with a neatness and finish which is destructive of many of the most noble and most salutary exercises of mind in the individual Christian. That feeling of awe and piety which the mysteriousness of the Gospel should excite fades away under this fictitious illumination which is poured over the entire Dispensation. Criticism, we know, is commonly considered fatal to poetic fervour and imagination; and in like manner this technical religion destroys the delicacy and reverence of the Christian mind.

The thesis that I have been developing is, in short, that analysis is not a technique for comprehending an artwork, but rather an instrument for communicating an element of something which has already been comprehended; my point is that a more nearly adequate approach to the communication of the total work, and not just an aspect of it, is the creation of a climate of metaphor around the object by means of which it is gradually revealed. This creation of what might be paradoxically termed a "discursive poem" has the advantage of communicating not only the rational elements but those which I have called trans-rational as

well. No doubt in grasping the art object there is implicitly and synoptically some analysis, but the actual paths
which the intellect and sensibility pursue in this act of
comprehension are so multiform and devious, so uniquely
personal, so subtle and "omnigenous," that they cannot
be reduced to a single pattern or process. Those aspects
of comprehension which do admit of such reduction are
a few general rules, a few general principles (e.g., those
of scansion) the value of which in grasping this or that
concrete artifact is, by reason of their very generality, at
best merely propaedeutic: that is, when these principles
are not—as in fact they often are—irrelevant and distract-
ing, they are only of incidental worth. Analysis has the
relation to an artwork that a description of a kiss over the
telephone has to the real thing.

But before discussing the communication of the poem,
it is necessary to treat of the trans-rational elements in particular. In this context it is interesting to note that whereas
for Aristotle (VI, 14) finish of diction is regarded as attainable by neophytes, and as far inferior to a skill in constructing plots, for Longinus, diction is an essential and a
prime factor in achieving the sublime; similarly when Aristotle remarks that poetry implies either a happy gift of
nature or a strain of madness (XVII, 2), it is not difficult to
realize that this is a normative judgment, and that the
latter of the two implicits is less noble. This stands in contrast to Longinus' statement (VIII, 3) "I would affirm
with confidence that there is no tone so lofty as that of
genuine passion, in its right place, when it bursts out in a
wild gust of mad enthusiasm and as it were fills the
speaker's words with frenzy." In chapter XXXIX, when
Longinus discusses the fifty elements which contribute
to the sublime, he speaks of the harmonious arrangement

of words as "a wonderful instrument of lofty utterance and of passion." He continues:

> For does not the flute instil certain emotions into its hearers and as it were make them beside themselves and full of frenzy, and supplying a rhythmical movement constrain the listener to move rhythmically in accordance therewith and to conform himself to the melody, although he may be utterly ignorant of music? Yes, and the tones of the harp, although in themselves they signify nothing at all, often cast a wonderful spell, as you know, over an audience by means of the variations of sounds, by their pulsation against one another, and by their mingling in concert. And yet these are mere semblances and spurious copies of persuasion, not (as I have said) genuine activities of human nature. Are we not, then, to hold that composition (being a harmony of that language which is implanted by nature in man and which appeals not to the hearing only but to the soul itself), since it calls forth manifold shapes of words, thoughts, deeds, beauty, melody, all of them born at our birth and growing with our growth, and since by means of the blending and variation of its own tones it seeks to introduce into the minds of those who are present the emotion which affects the speaker and since it always brings the audience to share in it and by the building of phrase upon phrase raises a sublime and harmonious structure: are we not, I say, to hold that harmony by these selfsame means allures us and invariably disposes us to stateliness and dignity and elevation and every emotion which it contains within itself, .gaining absolutely mastery over our minds?

This is a long text—in which Longinus himself attempted stylistically to exemplify his doctrine—but it does serve to indicate that whereas with Aristotle the devices of diction were often dangerous distractions from the all important plot ("Diction is to be elaborated in the pauses of the action.") to be employed decoratively, as vulgar concession, for enticing the inattentive, with Longinus they

85

were necessary and ennobling, precisely because they do gain "absolute mastery over our minds," that is, because they involve an ecstatic "abdication of reason."

If this sounds like the language of the romantic esthetic, of the enraptured impressionist critic, it does because it should. No one can doubt that Quiller-Couch, or Saintsbury, or Mark van Doren comprehended as much in the poem as such of our cooler contemporaries as Tate, or Wimsatt, or Kermode. No one can doubt that Edmund Gosse or William Lyon Phelps could read as well as the next man, or that Housman's beard or Dickinson's pate reacted to what any other hardheaded reader would have found equally—though perhaps more or less dermatically —moving. The error lay in viewing such uniquely personal experiences as criticism. William Lyon Phelps in his *Browning* covers nearly every major poem in what is almost a tour de force of fatuity. The method combines paraphrase with breathless excitement: seated on his tripod before the Yale undergraduates, William Lyon Phelps riddled the leaves of his text with as much diligence as Cleanth Brooks did some decades later. But criticism, like all philosophizing, as Kierkegaard said, is tautology. The difference between the new critics and the old, between Professor Brooks and Professor Phelps is that the one is tautologizing the poem, the other is tautologizing his response: both are laudable activities. But they have different names.

There are, it may be said, three trans-rational elements in a lyric, two of which are present also in the drama, and all of which have analogues in the various other art forms, painting, sculpture, music, and dance. The two which may be found in all poetic works are meter and what may be designated as the "daimonic word." The third, ultimate individuality, which is the *haecceitas* and inscape of Scotus and Hopkins, are pre-eminentally though not exclusively lyrical. I will take them now in order.

John Crowe Ransom has observed that "critics generally never offer enough of a theory about the meters ... there seems to have been a singular lapse of the critical imagination."[34] But even Mr. Ransom, when raising meter to the high condition of one of the three basic constructs in a poem, offers only a brief descriptive explanation of its function and some important but fragmentary hints on its nature. This singular lapse of the critical imagination on the part of one of our singularly imaginative critics itself suggests that there can be in the strict sense of the word no such *theory*. For an Aristotelian this critical lacuna is trivial because such embellishments are merely the spume that plays upon the plot of things. Though possibly Aristotle has said the last word in his statement, "There is an instinct for harmony and rhythm, meters being manifestly sections of rhythm." (It is a philosophical convenience to explain our needs by some instinctive want: this is the heresy of periphrasis.)

In this question of meters, one cannot talk simply about poetic beat operative, as mnemonic device, as exemplified in the works of Poe and Lanier (Emerson's "jingle men"), nor simply about the alleged desirability of using this or that particular foot for this or that particular dramatic effect. One can only talk about the *body* of the words, about their physical texture, about their impact on the ear and on the blood stream, about their quantity, about the mystery they support, and the entrancement they engender. This is not to talk about words flowing into image, into symbol, and finally, into gesture and behavior; that would be the word already informed by a kind of soul; perhaps not entirely a rational soul, but in any event, a life principle. For present purposes one must conceive imaginatively the impossible possibility of the word as so richly physical that it can be grasped by the intellect only.

It is a remarkable phenomenon that rhythm and meter, which are common to all poetry, and from which poetry probably took its origins, are among the most inexplicable elements of the poem. Eliot and most modern critics, following Hopkins' line of thought, see metered language as imposing another pattern, sometimes paralleling the meaning and sometimes independent of it, upon the native rhythms, with the poem as a congregation—attending to the homiletic plot—of various shuffling feet: an explanation which, as Graves rightly noted, explains nothing, and involves a process comparable to putting water into the gasoline tank of a car in order to make it go by fits and starts. Graves himself, whose poetry almost invariably is in traditional forms, has a characteristically ingenious anthropological theory which takes the traditional conception of rhythm as rooted in our longing for order (e.g., in the diastole and systole, the seasonal cycle, the rise and setting of the sun, etc.) and gives it a sharp antiquarian twist. The rhythms of our poetry are the heirs of the measured beats of the Scandinavian sea-rovers' oars and of the tread of the hierophant in the mystery rituals. We of the present are presumably moved by similar rhythms because we have not only our own generation in our bones, but bear about with us as well—like the original sin—these pulsations from the past.

I would suggest that the meters operate in a manner similar to that of rhyme and linguistic collision discussed above. Primarily the metered language represents the ordering of chaos; it, too, puts the silver dew upon the mud. Like alliteration and other sonic devices it distracts us from the literal, factual, prose meaning and translates us into a world of harmony. It may of course parallel the state-ment as in good prose or in dramatic poetry. But in the lyric it lives a kind of private life of its own in the com-panionship not of the rational plot but of those other trans-rational elements being discussed here. Why, then, bother about the paraphrasable factual statement itself? Why not settle for the music of the "ultimate Plato," skip the mean-ings entirely and enjoy only the meters? Bypassing the obvious reason that poetry is verbal and that words by definition have definitions, the reason is that to be a media-tor one has to be in touch with both extremes *at once*. The meters are sonically what paradox is structurally, and what metaphor is figuratively: the arabesque which weaves between the worlds of Aristotle and Plato, between the definite and the infinite.

But whatever the explanation may be, one thing is cer-tain: meter and rhythm do move us in a manner which does not, beyond some rudimentary lessons, admit of rational analysis.

So, too, with what may be called the "daimonic word," or the word as "soul." Soul I here define as something similar to that vital principle which according to the medie-val theory informed the human foetus: in this notion, which has since been abandoned on theological grounds, the unborn infant was animated successively by a threptic and an esthetic soul, before a dianoetic soul was introduced to engender a truly human being. Now a word embraces, as it were these less evident senses, and has hiding behind its rational meaning a secret substructure, which, though we cannot identify it, does nevertheless fall under the power of the intellect. Few would question that even for modern man, words do have a quasi-magic force, and that words, seemingly by themselves, do have a captivating power: witness Shakespeare, whose puns are rarely structural and

89

cannot be explained merely in terms of the Renaissance
delight in verbal oddities. Our greatest poet, and a poet
who often seemed to want what any good burgher or
country gentleman might want, could not resist the enchantment of the word-play.

All figures to illustrate the word as "soul" are deficient,
though one is tempted to introduce the iceberg image to
convey the picture of secret, undisclosed depths. Perhaps
a better analogy would be that of prismatic rays, the
word, then, being composed of the whole range of colors
which, though present, are not visible; hence the poet,
himself somewhat of a rationalist, and a decrier of embellishments, could write:[35]

> False eloquence, like the prismatic glass
> Its gaudy colours spreads on ev'ry place.

If one were to denominate the pure white light as the rational element that we are immediately conscious of, and the
rest of the spectrum as expressive of the non-rational elements that only *intellectus* can comprehend, it is obvious
that the peculiar beauty of a great deal of poetry is denied
to those critics who are blinded by reason and who can
recognize, therefore neither the ultra-violets nor the infra-
reds, the alphas nor the omegas.

For example, a well-blanched critical statement runs as
follows:[36]

> We are in fact *far less* moved by the words as mere words
> than we think; we think ourselves moved mainly by them
> because they are the only visible or audible part of the poem.
> As soon as we grasp the grammatical meaning of an expression
> in a mimetic poem, we begin drawing inferences which we
> scarcely recognize as inferences, because they are just such
> as we *habitually* make in life: inferences from the speech as
> to the character, his situation, his thought, his passion, sud-

denly set the speaker vividly before us and arouse our
emotions in sympathy or antipathy; our humanity is engaged,
and it is engaged by humanity. But where we can draw no
such inferences, where no such impression of humanity is
conveyed, we remain *largely* indifferent in the face of the
finest diction. These inferences, moreover, largely determine
our interpretation of the language itself; we recognize a pun
or an ambiguity when we see a human reason why the
character should deal in puns and ambiguities, and not when
the dictionary lists a variety of meanings. [italics added]

There is a good deal of verbal hedging here which makes
this seemingly brave ultimatum to Empson turn out in
sum to be quite modest: in fact the type of ambiguity the
above comments employs verges on the diploid. The under-
scored adverbs give the statement this double shift, so
that one is never quite sure whether or not Professor
Olson concedes the possibility of *some* trans-rational element in the word. But if we are "far *less* moved by the
words as mere words than *we think* (sic)," and if we "remain *largely* indifferent in the face of the finest diction"
it is self-evident that we are *somewhat* moved by the words
as mere words and that we remain *somewhat* un-indifferent
in the face of the finest diction. There is then *something*
in the words and diction, entirely apart from the meaning, to which we respond. If this something is slightly present in some poems, it can be dominantly present in others;
and it is the contention here that those "others" make up
that poetic family we call lyric. But to maintain the existence of a trans-rational word, as this essay has done, is
not to deny that the "grammatical meaning" may be primary in drawing our attention to the word itself. After
all, the only way into the inside is through the outside.

But the lyric is understatement which is overheard. On
the elementary level, as I have noted, this means simply
that it is not an incitement to action, but an object of

contemplation. However, in a deeper sense it means that it is the reduction, the diminution, of the universal to the concrete, which is the work of metaphor and personification. The poet is not concerned that youths can't leap brooks, but that all boys die. So too:[37]

> And I shall find some girl perhaps,
> And a better one than you,
> With eyes as wise, but kindlier,
> And lips as soft, but true.

Only a fetishistic deviate would read this as statement.

Every name word is, then, the understatement of the eternal logos; every image is the defining of the infinite *Urbild*. The hills are, as Hopkins said, His world-heaving shoulders. The word seeks to pass beyond its dictionary meaning to the transcendent. Understatement is not quite pure apophasis, poetry is not quite mysticism: it is not quite the path of knowledge by not-knowing, the via negativa. But neither is it the way of simple affirmation of philosophers. Poetry mediates these two realms. "The light that never was on sea or land," is like the light and the sea and the land we know, and at the same time it is, Wordsworth explicitly tells us, *completely different* from them.

What Professor Olson, like most theorists on the drama, is usually talking about is an *approximation* of poetry, that is, a purer form of prose. With the currency of prose one gets exactly what one pays for; with the coinage of poetry one rents the gingerbread castle or buys a ticket to the concert of the spheres. Prose is the language of the univocal fact; poetry is the language which reaches beyond the fact to the primary factor. One doesn't have to put Shakespeare the lyricist of the early plays into competition with Shakespeare the dramatist of the great tragedies, though it is perhaps as true of him as of others that, as Cardinal Newman said, the process of development consisted in putting off the poetry of childhood for the prose of old age. But Shakespeare remains, even in the period of the great tragedies, a lyric genius, and therefore it is of no great critical moment if Professor Olson thinks "we recognize a pun or an ambiguity when we see a human reason why the character should deal in puns and ambiguities." This raises only the question of Olson's ability to read the plays and is of no speculative importance here; though, one would like to see him exercise his theory by integrating these ambiguities—"the bitter-sweet of this Shakespearean fruit," as E. A. Robinson called them—into the dramatic action. This would entail, one feels, a multiple préciosité of technique that would make Empson with his relatively clumsy niceties appear as a simple child crying, "O Master! we are seven."

Really what "human reason" can there be in Shakespeare to explain that compulsive dealing in "puns and ambiguities" which so disturbed Dr. Johnson, another neo-Aristotelian—and also a lexicographer? It may be suggested that the pun represents an effort on the part of the word to escape its definition, to reach out beyond its literal fixed meaning and thus to be more like the logos in whom all meanings are contained. Keats is consciously attempting to suggest that the pun is mightier than the word as defined by dictionaries when he offers as balm for the beloved's anger, the advice: "And feed deep, deep upon her peerless eyes." It is not merely that these are, as the dictionary would have it, eyes beyond compare; they are also the sightless eyes—eyes that cannot peer—of ideal woman who knows and understands, who grasps reality blindly, by feeling. They are at once the eyes of Aristotelian Fanny and of the Platonic eternal feminine. In this sense the

93

ambiguity of the pun is an attempt to reveal the word's transcendental relation with that Word which in theology is the exemplary cause of all things.

And in fact do we not find ourselves so moved by the "finest diction" that we instinctively repudiate Hazlitt on the author of "Kubla Khan," "Mr. Coleridge can write better nonsense verses than anyone else in England"? In "Kubla Khan" there is no *rational* engagement of our humanity, and yet our response to the poem is one of delight, possibly because reason is not the only faculty for engaging our humanity, and possibly because, as Raissa Maritain has shown, nonsense often makes more sense than sense: and this because this sense beyond sense is attained by that transcending of reason which is the office of intellect. In the following stanza[38]

> No nightingale did ever chaunt
> More welcome notes to weary bands
> Of travellers in some shady haunt,
> Among Arabian sands:
> A voice so thrilling ne'er was heard
> In springtime from the cuckoo bird,
> Breaking the silence of the seas
> Among the farthest Hebrides.

—lines 3 and 4 have the same "dramatic" function as lines 7 and 8; both couplets are expressions of some ultimate degree of remotion and perfection, and they provide the foil which illustrates the superiority of the more proximate chant of the maiden. (This would seem to be "humanistic" criticism as they define it at Chicago: we even have the suitable number of latinisms to qualify it as "reasoned discourse.") Elaborate and amplify these remarks, coordinate them with similar observations on the remaining lines, mix in a few comments on "total structure," "composite continuum," "whole contexts," insinuate an attack on the "new" criticism, and one has pretty well got up the neo-Aristotelian recipe. But it seems to most readers that one of the most moving (i.e., "engaging the humanity") aspects of this poem is in the last two lines of the stanza above:

> Breaking the silence of the seas
> Among the farthest Hebrides.

Cleveland's Hebrides do not so move us:[39]

> As that our tears shall seem the Irish Seas,
> We floating islands, living Hebrides.

Nor do Milton's:[40]

> ...where ere thy bones are hurl'd
> Whether beyond the stormy Hebrides
> Where thou perhaps under the whelming tide
> Visit'st the bottom of the monstrous world

Nor do Coleridge's lines, which Wordsworth here is echoing:[41]

> And we did speak only to break
> The silence of the sea.

There is in these lines of Wordsworth a sense of infinite longing—of existential pathos, I would say—of anguish for union with an absolute, which is simply not disclosed by rational analysis, and which is not derived from the rational statement as such, for why should not Arabian sands express spaciousness and isolation (if spaciousness and isolation be a concomitant of what we are talking about) as

**95**

well as the farthest Hebrides? Nor is it enough to say this couplet synthesizes the tenor of the whole poem which suggests boundless projection: the vale overflowing, the song possibly meaningless, seemingly endless, and timeless, "What has been and may be again"—all of which elements have been stressed by Professors Wimsatt and Pottle and by Dom Sebastian Moore. Nor is the language deliquescent or vaporously romantic. And why the focus on these two lines? The Hebrides may be the farthest limit of Britain, but they are nevertheless a defined, localized point. Shelley might have written "Beyond the farthest Pleiades," and we would have had a paraphrasable content suggestive of infinity. Cleveland's rhythm is more emphatically falling than Wordsworth's.

Beyond this, analysis cannot go. One can account for this sense of vastation only in terms of the concealed substructure of this verbal configuration, in which reside the "magic" roots, the trans-rational and the physiological parts of the word.

Finally, I come to the last element of the triad: the unique individuality of the lyric poem. It has already been stressed that the lyric is the poem of the *concrete* universal, of image rather than of action. It is the poem, to quote Hopkins, for which "some matter and meaning is essential, but only as an element necessary to support and employ the shape which is contemplated for its own sake:" a shape which is harmonized and ordered by the highest reaches of spirit—logos, and which may be in complete opposition to the cacophonous and fragmented nature of the subject matter or plot of the particular lyric in question. It is not the poem of pure sensation (as with Hugo Bluemner's collocations of sounds or as with the Paris advocates of Lettrisme) because matter does not exist apart from form. But it is a poetry the form of which is not constituted by rational content (Aristotle's "soul of tragedy" was a *rational* soul).

These patterns of speech, which are the defining trait of the lyric, exist in a greater tension than does the slack speech of everyday affairs; these patterns which are so rooted in the thickest materiality, and at the same time are so impregnated to their deepest depth by the most ardent spirit, create that dialectic thrust towards pure Spirit which we all undergo when encountering them. And it is this same colliding union of infinite and definite that makes the occasion of these utterances experiences of anguish and aspiration. Because matter as such says muteness, because spirit as such transcends all verbal articulation, in the presence of such experiences we can only be silent: it is then that the silence speaks.

The intellectual knowledge of singulars receives a singularly obscure treatment in most tracts of Aristotelian-Scholastic psychology. The very materiality of the individual thing inhibits our understanding of it, because, as St. Thomas says, "nothing is understood except immaterially." But it is curious to note in passing that the process whereby we come to know the singular, in this philosophical tradition, entails a kind of poetic activity, and this not in the obvious sense of the *nous poietikos* (the agent intellect) as a creative force, but rather in the sense that our knowledge of the individual is achieved by a mysterious reflection of the intellect upon the phantasm: what is begotten from this reflection is a kind of "concrete universal."

But if the singular resists being known by reason of its very materiality, how much more resistance will not be evident when it is a question of that which pleonastically may be said to be absolutely and uniquely "singular," that which may be said to be the optimum expression of individuality? What is being suggested here is that each lyric struggles against being comprehended rationally, and that we should approach each individual poem not with some pattern of universally applicable rules for its dissection, but with an attitude of complete acquiescence in its particular and unique nature. Each lyric poem is, as it were, like each angel and constitutes therefore a kind of species to itself. To paraphrase and adapt St. Thomas, "There are as many lyric species as there are individual lyrics." Of course, this is to exaggerate slightly in order to point up the utter individuality of the lyric in contrast to the relative and more universalized individuality of the drama.

Now given these trans-rational elements, how can one speak meaningfully of the poetic object? The question as it is posed here is pedagogical (though it may seem from what follows that it is mystagogical) rather than critical. There is no concern at this point with assessing the merits of a particular artifact so much as with communicating what has already been grasped as admirable. The question, then, as I said in the beginning, is: Can the humanities be taught?

Man embraces the total significance of an artwork as he embraces the total person of his beloved. When a man comprehends the unique character of his beloved, he does not do so at the end of a detailed analytic process; rather he simply possesses the person of the beloved, in all its goodness, beauty, and concrete reality in one synoptic intuition. Such an intuition may, of course, be the result of a long period of contemplation. But this is precisely where all methodologies of appreciation, all yogisms for comprehending the uniquely human necessarily fail: they seek too much, too rapidly, and by the wrong route.

Every true poem, it has been here maintained, is a

mystery; it is, as the going terminology affirms, something *sacred*. It cannot be grasped like a problem by analysis, but it can be communicated, as I have already suggested, by constructing around it a climate of metaphor. I cited earlier some words of Newman relating religious attitudes to poetry, and we have all grown accustomed to the kinds of combinations such as "poetry and prayer" that I have discussed in the preceding essay. I would like to quote another passage from Newman in which he parallels the role of the teacher with that of oral tradition in the communication of religious truth.[42]

> ... its great instrument, or rather organ, has ever been that which nature prescribes in all education, the personal presence of a teacher, or, in theological language, Oral Tradition. It is the living voice, the breathing form, the expressive countenance, which preaches, which catechizes. Truth, a subtle, invisible, manifold spirit, is poured into the mind of the scholar by his eyes and ears, through his affections, imagination, and reason.

Since we are concerned with pedagogical questions he pertinence of this text is obvious. But it should be said that the Church relies not only on oral tradition but on the liturgy as well in the preservation and elucidation of doctrine, as the axiom, *lex credendi, lex orandi* points up. The liturgy as worship renews the redemptive act of Christ; but the liturgy as catechesis takes into account that man cannot fully realize the deeper significance of the mystery of redemption, and, therefore, around this one central religious reality it constructs, as it were, a ring of lesser mysteries celebrated in the temporal and sanctoral cycles. Around the great poem of God-become-man, the church celebrates the derivative poems of the daily feasts. For good reason then, did Maurice Zundel entitle his most celebrated work *Le Poème de la sainte liturgie.*

Every poem is mystery, (that is, metaphor) and can be communicated only by the creation around it of a climate of derivative, lesser, subsidiary metaphors (that is, mysteries). To make use of a more homely parable, it could be said that just as the young person does not go about with a list of desirable traits to use as a standard for relating his I-ness to another's Thou-ness, that is, for finding a mate, neither does he, when in love, imagine that any catalog of qualities can explain the loveliness of the beloved. But he does write a poem, or more than likely a sequence of poems. And so, too, the pedagogue: around the particular poem, around the central mystery being publicly contemplated he constructs under the power of his emotional response a series of lesser poems, of diffused poems, of, one might say, prose poems, which refract the clear-obscure light of the core poem.

From this pedagogical viewpoint, as has already been indicated, one may wonder whether the disdain and distaste often manifested by newer critics such as Leavis and Kermode for older critics such as Quiller-Couch or William Lyon Phelps has been properly focussed; the critical writings of the latter may represent a blending of emotion with paraphrase, but, as already suggested, there is every reason to believe that by and large their responsoria were as sensitive and as finely adjusted as those of any modern critics, and that as pedagogues they were as effective as any of the contemporary advocates of the new orthodoxy—or the new paradoxy. And even from the standpoint of criticism a man like Quiller-Couch, with his maverick standards, with his Johnsonian dogmatism, with his unverifiable yet irrefutable judgments, represents —the *Scrutiny* fulminations notwithstanding—a healthy phenomenon in the arts: and so does Mr. Yvor Winters. Critics such as "Q" stand for the primacy of the individual judgment over any measurable standards or criteria, and they provide those evaluations of excellence that people like Karl Shapiro and Graham Hough cannot discover in the corpus of modern criticism.

This argument, then, is not directed against any employment of the various batteries of critical technique, but against their exclusive, self-reliant, presumptuous employment.

It is necessary to add, rather self-consciously, that one hopes the following will not seem too effusive; if it does *seem* so, this should probably be attributed to our native reticence, which is possibly as much an outgrowth of Jansenism as of Puritanism, when faced with any affective issue. For it must be recognized, from the beginning, that one has to be in love with the art object as one must be in love with any humane reality, and only then will the fulness of being radiate out from that object. All aspects of being tend to diffuse themselves. Beauty tends of its nature to go out of itself, and man possessing being in a conscious way tends to go out of himself and encounter this beauty, embrace this beauty, and share his being, his inner personal beauty, with the beauty of the object. This is the true meaning of *ekstasis*, the movement from oneself towards the object. In this moment of mutual sharing, the object is no longer "object"—that which is projected outside the self—for object and subject, without quite losing their separate identities, are interfused. And *ekstasis* is consummated.

Hence, again in the overused terminology of Marcel, the relation of subject and object is one of mystery. Mystery is any relation to being which impinges upon and absorbs one's very self; it is a relation the meaning of which cannot be adequately reduced to external terms, that is, which, by definition does not admit of "reasoned discourse." Mys-

101

tery demands union. Problem, which is any relation in which subject and object remain detached and divorced, implies permanent separation. Now, in the light of these observations, a critic can neither say that he is going to study an artwork objectively, nor, paradoxically, can he talk meaningfully of the objective "meaning" of it. The critic who regards the poem as a problem to be solved, as an object to be analyzed, never touches the inner core of the poetic creation; ignoring Debussy's principle that what the fusing genius of the artist has joined together must never be separated, such a critic can merely manipulate the various living elements of the poem, and devote himself to embalming its corpse in some prose description or paraphrase.

One might at this juncture draw another parallel from the religious tradition: it is universally accepted by spiritual writers that the various methods of "mental prayer," authored by such masters as St. Ignatius Loyola or M. Olier, do not guarantee contemplation; there can be no such guarantee, and this, not only because contemplation requires a supernatural grace, but because the purpose of these methods is merely to prepare, to condition the mind for praying. On the contrary, what is often taught in our schools as critical methodology is not regarded as a device for familiarizing the student with the peripheries of poetry and the arts: what is taught is *the* way for "understanding poetry." Methods of mental prayer fulfill the same function in the realm of religious contemplation that the kind of extra-curricular training, provided by many schools, in dancing and in the social graces, fulfills in the order of human love: a very minor preparatory role, only obliquely linked to the object towards which such technique may be directed. Yet the rationalist methods that are taught in many schools for the "understanding" of art works are similar to a shamanistic training in mystical contemplation, or to instruction in techniques for what is barbarously called "love making."

From the viewpoint of the Christian tradition, as well as from the viewpoint of most humanists who are not conscious agnostics, there are five aspects of spirit, all analogically related, to which men can be bound in an interior union: God, who is absolute being; man, who participates consciously in being; and truth, goodness, and beauty which are transcendental properties or aspects of being. Now a bond with any of these cannot be the direct result of some activity in the order of technique, because being has a natural affinity with being itself, and not with any artificial nexus that man may construct to force this bond. Thus it is the God whose absolute being is his nature that man loves; it is not any abstract theological definition nor any verbal conception—though these may have their great value—to which man is related. Similarly when a person loves another person, in the temporal order, it is not the exterior traits, nor the sum of all the qualities, that are loved but the physical-spiritual person in all his ontological and paradoxical richness. So, too, in the comprehension of a profound truth: for the more profound a truth is, the more it shares in being, and the less capable it is of complete comprehension by the technical instruments of logic. Hence the realization of first principles cannot be the product of deduction because they are immediately seized in that natural juncture of being with being which engenders meaning.

In every encounter with being one recognizes an element that cannot be verbalized; for one makes in any relation with being or its properties an ontological response, the original utterance of which is denigrated by later efforts to bring it into the logical order. What then must the teacher do in attempting to arouse his students to an awareness of this transcendental and trans-rational aspect in things? Certainly he must not dispense with all canons of criticism, examination, and verification, and substitute for them a vague emotionalism; and certainly, too, he must not be driven to stammer like the mystic in a vain attempt at expressing the ineffable.

Without setting aside the traditional instruments for measuring and analyzing some facet of his particular discipline, the teacher of the humanities must realize the inadequacy of these instruments in bringing about a genuine communion with the object, and he must realize that any exclusively technical method, however subtle and refined, cannot produce this mysterious union of being with being. He must realize further that no matter how desirable on democratic or egalitarian grounds it may be to develop a technique that will reduce the arcana of the spiritual sciences to a popular understanding, such a desideratum remains—through technique alone—unattainable.

The teacher may depend initially on analysis, but he must rely finally, for this ultimate educational achievement, on a highly personalized reflection over the body of truth or beauty being considered. In this way his own insight becomes the instrument for awakening a consciousness of their being within his students; which consciousness, when it is aroused, is then capable of responding to the being in all reality. Such a highly personalized and poetic reflection will be necessarily diffuse and repetitious, for, while the mystery of reality cannot be perfectly exhausted by logical instruments alone, it can in a sense be encompassed and thus imperfectly assimilated by rhetoric.

And this rhetorical expression will be, in turn, metaphoric rather than descriptive. Description tells what a thing does; metaphor conveys what a thing is. Descriptive analysis is concerned with the products of a thing, and with the effects flowing from its collision with other things; description, then, is concerned primarily with doing and has a large role to play in teaching the drama or, for that matter, any other rational discipline. Rhetorical metaphor is concerned with creating a format of ambient symbols and parables which, in its dependence on every facet of life and experience, in its reliance on a *Gestalt* of images drawn from all elements in the universe, predisposes to a kind of revelation of the thing itself: the encounter with being. Nothing, of course, can ever guarantee the revelation of the poem. In the realm of spirit there is never any absolute assurance of attainment. But if, to put it baldly, poetry is spiritual and prose is material, then the way to grasp a poem must not be by prose, but can only be by another poem.

Descriptive language is language derived from a material instrument employed upon the object; it is the language of those who hold the object, as it were, at arm's length, and who are anxious to keep the object remote and detached. The result of such a disengaged examination, when it culminates in nothing higher is to objectivize the person himself—a condition one recognizes in many rationalists who, however talented and professionally adept they may be, appear personally stunted and dwarfed. That relation to the object whereby one "ingathers" all subordinate "objective" knowledge so that such knowledge is no longer a mere collocation of data, a mere assemblage of facts, but is literally "oneself" and is grasped as one grasps one's own selfness—that relation, in the strict sense of the phrase, "beggars description." Description, as I have noted implies a circuit, a movement around the object—as the expression, "to *describe* a circle," would indicate. Description is the language of exteriority: and the more it is exclusively em-

105

ployed, the more it tends to exteriorize the person. But metaphor is the language of interiority; it is the language of the communion of being with being; that is, it is the language of mystery, of love.

Because metaphor is the language of love (whether one thinks of the rudest expressions, e.g., "sweetheart," "honey," or of the greatest poetry) it is also the language of spontaneity. The choice of words is not premeditated; the structure of words is not pre-arranged; but neither are they left to hazard, to indetermination. Metaphoric language is dictated by the teacher's encounter and union with the being of the reality he is contemplating. Certainly one prepares specific remarks and comments, and certainly, too, one's descriptions are prepared. But at that moment when in the presence of the object, one is moved to speech by its beauty or by the depths of truth it discloses, at that moment when takes place the marriage of subject and object, and when occurs the educational act itself, at that moment, the teacher is, in the ancient sense of the word, an "enthusiast." He is moved as it were, from on high; he is inspired, and he speaks the language of spirit which is metaphor. It is to this that Claudel refers:[43]

In the case of those verities whose evidence or reality is thrust upon him without his intelligence being able to grasp them whole, or see through them, it can proceed by way of logical deduction. This is done equally by science and scholastic philosophy, which is a quasi-grammatical interpretation of the real. Or else it can take its stand before this known-unknown in a state of freshness, good faith, candour, virginity, absolute sincerity, as well as impassioned attention .... He will substitute for pure logical deduction (though not rejected and though left in its place of eminence, and besides, no instrument is one too many) a sort of ... topography.... Mysteries explain themselves less by themselves

than by explaining all the rest as a lamp is proved less by its
wick than by its light.

With the advent of various personalist philosophies it
is growing less easy to mock this creation of a climate of
metaphor as so much emotional fantasy. That passage from
Gibbon's journal cited at the beginning of this paper represents as empiric a fact as the upshot of any bundle of
syllogisms, and it bears repetition here:

> Till now, I was acquainted only with two ways of criticiz-
> ing a beautiful passage: the one to show, by an exact anatomy
> of it, the distinct beauties of it, and from whence they sprung;
> the other, an idle exclamation, or a general encomium,
> which leaves nothing behind it. Longinus has shown me that
> there is a third. He tells me his own feelings upon reading
> it; and tells them *with such energy* that he communicates
> them. I almost doubt which is the most sublime, Homer's
> battle of the gods, or Longinus's apostrophe to Terentianus
> upon it.

Professor McKeon reads this as advocating a kind of
Arnoldian touchstone and a poetic *consensus fidelium:* in
judging artworks, and gives to it the felicitous title, "rhetorical criterion of insight and agreement." [44] One might
preferably accent here the Longinian notion of intuitive
spontaneity, and one may then use the language of Berenson in describing the artist as wit: [45]

> Almost unconscious and even surprised to hear what comes
> out of his own mouth, he utters the winged words, the un-
> forgettable phrase .... Like every other artist, he welcomes
> and enjoys applause, but the most determining reason for his
> action is that under certain circumstances he cannot resist
> the impulse to talk brilliantly ....

It is when the mind of the teacher is in full activity that
those insights born of the "ingathering," born of the

union with the object, become vocal. For this reason Bishop Söderblom has observed of the first great teacher, ". . . to Socrates the Daimonion was something that fell upon him when exercising his vocation, not something attainable by a methodic schooling and training of the mind."[46] Concerning such intuition and such expression, the first rule is that there is no first rule.[47]

> One's grand flights, one's Sunday baths,
> One's tootings at the weddings of the soul
> Occur as they occur.

Yet one can *condition* himself to verbalize these "grand flights."

Again an illustration from the life of prayer may be helpful: according to the great spiritual masters, the best preparation for mystical contemplation, for the prayer of simplicity—for "the weddings of the soul"—is not the proximate directing of the mind to God, but the habitual awareness of God's presence. So, too, the best preparation for this metaphoric expression will not be one's immediate attention to the object of contemplation—though, of course, this is indispensable—but as extensive knowledge, as habitual a consciousness of as wide a field of human endeavor as one can compass. If the intellect is "in a certain sense everything" then the educator must have as broad a knowledge as possible so that there will be resident within himself a universe of figures and symbols that will be evoked at the moment when the object playing upon his mind and sensibility is suddenly seized in its totality.

Just as the theologian will illuminate his doctrine by principles drawn from philosophy, from the contemplation of nature and art, and just as the scientist will bring the notions of physics, mathematics, and chemistry in convergence on the point he is elucidating, so, too, the great teacher of the arts, energized by humane emotion, must throw his images into another and another calculus of language in order that the transcendental and trans-rational object he is revealing may become more and more evident, until the planes of each succeeding expression he employs gradually take shape and the polygon of his utterance more and more approximates the circle of the object. The inscribed polygon will never identify itself with the circle: the object will never be completely encompassed: but man the knower will know as perfectly as his imperfect faculties allow.

# 3

## Poet, Metaphysician, and the Desire for God

EVEN before Plato, speaking as philosopher, exiled the poets from his ideal city, relations between the metaphysician and the poet had been strained. Of course, the poets would not have been at home in any ideal city anyway, since what they would prefer is not the ideal city nor the real city, but that city which merges both, and which may be said to float midway on the waves of being. The poet would prefer neither London with its chartered streets nor the heavenly Jerusalem of the ideated world, but the blending of the two in that matutinal vision when all things "are open unto the fields and unto the sky," when heaven and earth are made one.[1]

Since the Romantics the armed truce which had hitherto prevailed has broken out into a shooting war exemplified by Kierkegaard's harsh separation of the ethical from the esthetic and Goethe's condemnation of Scholasticism for its insensitivity to beauty. In the Romantic program philosophy would[2]

> clip an Angel's wings,
> Conquer all mysteries by rule and line,
> Empty the haunted air, and gnomed mine—
> Unweave a rainbow....

110

This bitter antipathy between metaphysician and poet has been extended into our time and continues unremittingly to govern what little intercourse takes place between the two. Though poets while writing prose may pay homage to philosophy, when being their better selves in the act of making poem, they invariably revert to form—or rather to form and matter together.

What makes the poetry of Wallace Stevens anomalous in its choice of subject is both its concern with adjudicating the quarrel between the two areas and its genuine respect for the work of the metaphysician, a respect which is surpassed only by that for the work of the poet: ". . . in spite of M. Jacques Maritain we do not want to be metaphysicians." [3] But the statement could never have been made if the achievement of Maritain the philosopher did not constitute a serious temptation for the poet. Nor is this surprising since both of them are seeking to order "words. . . . In ghostlier demarcations, keener sounds."[4] So preoccupied was Stevens with this theme of the possible confluence or rapprochement of art and metaphysics that it may be said to be the controlling idea of a major part of his opus. For Stevens, the recurrent ritual of man in which he finds solace is the making of poetry or the making of metaphysics. And although the poet in Stevens will occasionally deride the metaphysician, the more prevalent attitude is one of cordial rivalry or even of close association in mutually attempting the impossible.

It is this spirit of amicable competitiveness that dominates the short masterpiece, "Annual Gaiety," in which the philosopher is mocked for the pretentiousness of his all-inclusive claims and also for his inevitable failure:

> In the morning in the blue snow
> The Catholic sun, its majesty,
> Pinks and pinks the ice-hard melanchole.

The induction is rhythmically grandiloquent: surely a saving revelation is about to be handed down from the lectern, one feels—only to have one's hopes snapped up short by the realization that the "catholic" sun (the universalizing sun of prose in contrast to the twilighting moon of poetry) in all its splendor can only pink and pink the icy block of reality. The "men of sun/ And men of day"[5] cannot melt the block into the sacred river, cannot really give us as does the poet, "the life that is fluent in even the wintriest bronze;"[6] the philosopher can only transiently tint the surface of things. He does not embrace and wed himself to the universe; he does not "mate his life with life/ That is the sensual pearly spouse,"[7] but confines himself to "pinking" the object of his desire. The word, of course, is "pinch" and is reminiscent of the more traditionally Romantic sentiment of one of Stevens' contemporaries:[8]

> O sweet spontaneous
> earth how often have
> the
> doting
>    fingers of
> prurient philosophers pinched
> and
> poked
> thee

The grandiosity of the promises of philosophy and their invariable unfulfillment are brought out by the ironic collision of what we are led to anticipate from the *scientia rectrix* (*its* majesty: metaphysicians always priding themselves on the impersonalness of their universal truths) and the triviality of its actual achievement. But Stevens is not here decrying all metaphysics; he is not shrieking as did Blake—in his own unconscious paradox—"To generalize is to be an idiot"; he is only puncturing the philosopher's imperialist claims.

In the face of the metaphysicians' assumption that only they can attain truth, Stevens asks the obvious question: If metaphysics works, why write poems?

> Wherefore those prayers to the moon?
> Or is it that alligators lie
> Along the edges of your eye
> Basking in desert Florida?

But the answer to the question is so obvious that the poet does not defer to supplying it—poets unlike philosophers never providing us with catechisms. The alligators which are the amphibians dwelling in the dual worlds of fluency and solidity, water and land, are the true instruments of our salvation. They represent the fused paradox which, like Coleridge's water-snakes, gives us the power to merge opposites, to bless all things both *great* and *small*, and ultimately to have the "knowledge of *good* and *evil*," that is, of *spirit* and *matter*. But these alligators of Stevens are not just the poems swimming in the cold, companionable streams of being, are not just Mrs. Malaprop's "allegories" (though Mrs. Malaprop spoke only poetry, the ever malapropos because untimely and atemporal), but they are the alligators which swim along the glittering eye of the poet. They are not, then, just poems; they are the very instinct that drives man to make the poem, to seek to fuse together all things uncomely and broken. And therefore, though by direct statement they are said to be lying along the edges of the eye (floating midway on the waves of the aqueous humor), they are also by direct statement basking somewhere else. The magic casement, which for Keats was the poem opening up to us a new world, is here seen not as a particular poem, but as the eye itself—

the window-wind-eye open to the breath of spirit, to the aria of the logos. And the alligators rightly lie in the land of antinomies, in the desert of matter and death which is flowering with life and form.

We pray to the moon, not to the "prosaic light of day" [9] because our very nature is that of ambiguous twi-lighted creatures whose destiny is to experience the tension of spirit and matter, and by that very experience to be driven to attempt its resolution. It is this sopho-moric condition of which the wise philo-sopher is deprived—as the univocity of all his affirmations shows: "... he/ that has lost the folly of the moon becomes/ The prince of the proverbs of pure poverty." [10] This "prince" is known to metaphysicians as a "principle."

Without bothering to answer his questions, Stevens concludes with an invocation to the patron of the most abstracting of all philosophers.

> Père Guzz in heaven strum your lyre
> And chant the January fire
> And joy of snow and snow.

To be a metaphysician would seem to be sufficiently abstract by itself, but to be a French philosopher obsessed with *raison* and *clarté* is to be yet abstracted even more from life and reality; and finally to be a celibate philosopher dedicated to *raison* and *clarté* is to be involved in what improperly the Scholastics might have called "the third degree of abstraction." But *paulo maiora canamus*: there is a higher degree of remotion possible, and it is to be not a living, celibate, French philosopher, but the *spiritual* father in heaven of such a philosopher. For Père Guzz (whose name indicates that he makes a kind of music, *quodammodo musica*, like the "sweet moan" of poetry) is Padre Domingo Guzman, founder of the order

114

of the Dominicans whose great light was Thomas Aquinas, depicted by Fra Angelico with a radiant sun disc upon his —not unfittingly—solar plexus.

But Stevens thumbing his nose at the sire of Aquinas thumbing his lyre was not discrediting all the claims of philosophy: like the poet, the philosopher does dwell in a land of paradox (the January fire), and this fire, being that of Janus, does provide a kind of twi-light. But unlike the fire of the poet, as we have seen, the January fire can only temporarily tint the ice-hard mystery of things; it cannot melt it and give us the life that is fluent in the wintriest bronze. What we want is the hot and the cold at once, the fluency in the rigidity, and for this no unitary seasons of winter or summer can suffice. To pink and pink the ice-hard melanchole is only to provide us with "tinsel in February, tinsel in August." [11] But these are not the "solutions" of the poet who lives in the seasons of duality, of that true metaphor which we like "under the trees in autumn" and in spring.[12] Moreover, the metaphysician does not really want the solution sweet; he enjoys torturing himself with the same questions century after century, and so his chant is ever the same: the "joy of snow and snow." For Stevens metaphysics is only a perennial snow-job.

In "Homunculus et La Belle Étoile," Stevens treatment of the metaphysician is more cordial, though still gently disdainful. Homunculus is the little man who for abundant recompense speaks in large statements; he is literally a mannikin and has therefore the same relation to the authentic man that a model has to the completed project. But he, too, the poem goes on to note, may be touched by the light of poetry, by the vision which gives not just ab-

115

stractions, not just models, but abstractions *and* concretions, models *and* fulfillments.

> In the sea, Biscayne, there prinks
> The young emerald, evening star,
> Good light for drunkards, poets, widows,
> And ladies soon to be married.

This light, joining together heaven and earth, is a twi-light which blends-evens the high and the low. And it is a light that shines most beneficently on all those who are incomplete and destined for union. In this sense everyone is a homunculus, is a mannikin rather than a full man; but the drunkards, poets, widows, and ladies-soon-to-be-married sense their own imbalance and vacuity, whereas the metaphysician, the satisfied half-man is convinced his model world is the true world.

> By this light the salty fishes
> Arch in the sea like tree-branches
> Going in many directions
> Up and down.

As has already been suggested, when the poet seeks to fuse opposites he is attempting to fuse all reality, he is seeking to re-ligamentize the divided image; hence while the fishes are going towards opposite directions at once, in those two directions all and "many directions" are contained. By this light the fish figure forth the image of the one and the many, of the spirit and the matter, in its most traditional symbol: the living tree which is not to be found in the leaf, the blossom, *or* the bole, but in the unified multiplicity of trunk and branches. The fish, then, represent man who by embracing the opposites, the alpha *and* omega, the up *and* down, can embrace all things. And thus the poet, man in his fullest state, by a light kindred to that of

116

the belle étoile, "Patches the moon together in his room/ To his Virgilian cadences, up down/ Up down." [13] And Crispin, a true weaver of dualities, "conceived his voyaging to be/ An up and down between two elements,/ A fluctuating between sun and moon,/ A sally into gold and crimson forms." [14]

> This light conducts
> The thoughts of drunkards, the feelings
> Of widows and trembling ladies,
> The movements of fishes.

By this light all are conducted, that is, are brought to fruition, pass from the half-state of being models to the full state of being the model *plus* the reality, the abstract *plus* the concrete. But furthermore, if drunkards have divided thoughts (the steady self and the antic disposition), and widows and trembling ladies have divided feelings (Should it be yes or no?) and fishes have divided movements (up and down), then this light unifies-con-ducts the two thoughts of the drunkards, the two responses of the ladies, the two directions of the fishes into one. What all of the latter have in common is that they experience the duality of their existence, while homunculus is smug in his static unitary condition.

Stevens in the next stanza adjusts the diction so that it portrays the prim attitude of the philosopher who has never been enraptured by the "other," who has never submitted to the lure of the "thou," and who therefore, unlike the ladies, drunkards, and fishes, will never be caught, and will remain always alone, always all-one with himself. Homunculus is what Blake called the "human abstract," only a digest or summary of a man. The language of this stanza is the placid imperturbable speech affected by those who have never been overtaken by anyone:

How pleasant an existence it is
That this emerald charms philosophers,
Until they become thoughtlessly willing
To bathe their hearts in later moonlight,

What ought to be the ekstasis of ex-istence is to the metaphysician only a pleasantry. But then, even he is momentarily drawn out of himself; yet still as a philosopher employing only those faculties which are the incessant subject of his disquisitions: *thought*lessly *will*ing. The charm of the enchanting star, the carmen which it chants cannot free the metaphysician from the prison of his self; the ecstasy is never consummated in the summing up of the division in which "I" and "thou" merge. The moment of charming charism is for the divided image only a diversion: "This chaos will not be ended, The red and the blue house blended." [15] What ought to have been the metaphysician's Sunday bath is only a moment of bathing, what ought to have been his grand flight is earth-bound by afterthought, and what ought to have been his wedding of the soul, remains only a phase of his celibacy: "One's grand flights, one's Sunday baths, one's tootings at the weddings of the soul, occur as they occur." [16]

But for homunculus this does not occur *as* it occurs; there is no chance happening here, no break-out into freedom, there is only a planned and plotted instant of digression to be rationalized as relaxation from what Kant self-gratulatingly called the "herculean labor" of philosophy. Moonlight becomes a device for warding off the occupational hazard of metaphysicians, the nervous breakdown in which the reflection gets enamored of its reflections in endless mental ipsation. The philosophers entertain themselves

Knowing that they can bring back thought

> In the night that is still to be silent,
> Reflecting this thing and that,
> Before they sleep!

It is precisely because they are bent in on themselves that the philosophers cannot get out of themselves and be one with another: they are just too reflective. And as such they have no proper self of their own; they are merely the mirror of the world of chaotic matter in which they reside, the reflectors of "this thing and that."

> It is better that, as scholars
> They should think hard in the dark cuffs
> Of voluminous cloaks,
> And shave their heads and bodies.

The irony of the philosophers' situation lies in the fact that *as scholars* (scholé-leisure) they ought to be utterly free (leisure-licere) to fall in love with the "other," to be not the half-man, but the living metaphor. On the superficial level—the level of the man who is all surface, all outside with no proper interiority, no in *and* out, no "up *and* down"—where the metaphysicians operate, it *is* better that as scholars they should think hard: this is their proper work (so they think) to solve the "hard problems." And in the strict sense the problems of metaphysics are always "hard" because the world of the hard is the world of unitary matter, it is the world of the impenetrable and therefore of the dark. Metaphysics cannot melt this ice-hard world as can poetry, it cannot draw forth from this rock the waters of life, of that life which is fluent in even the wintriest bronze. Wrapped in density the metaphysicians cannot share in the life of another, cannot participate in the wedding of the soul; for "The interest of life is experienced by participating and by being part, not by observing nor by thinking." [17] As eunuchs they remain the

119

bystanders of reality; though bathed by the light of beauty —and bathing was for all ancient peoples a prelude to marriage—they cannot put on the marriage garment; as voyeurs they can only divert themselves with philosophy, a pre-eminently spectator sport. "Poor Buffo! [buffing the mirror of self] Look at the lavender [the blending of blue and red]/ And look your last and look still steadily,/ And say how it comes that you see/ Nothing but trash and that you no longer feel/ Her body quivering in the Floréal." [18] Cloaked as they are by the dead letter of past systems and shrouded by the many volumes of their predecessors, the metaphysicians' thinking is always turned inwards.

But

> It might well be that their mistress
> Is no gaunt fugitive phantom.
> She might, after all, be a wanton,
> Abundantly beautiful, eager,
>
> Fecund,
> From whose being by starlight, on sea-coast,
> The innermost good of their seeking
> Might come in the simplest of speech.

What "might well be" would be the true well-being of the metaphysician; but what they *think* they want is not an other, a "thou," but only a duplicate of themselves, and therefore as model men, they want only the model woman, the abstract and unitary phantom. Even Wordsworth who toyed at metaphysics realized that the phantom of delight (the pure spiritual idea) must be fused with the "machine" (the absolute concretion) in the "creature not too bright or good/ For human nature's daily food." The true "other" for the metaphysician as for the poet is not the human aspect, but the full enfleshed woman, the spiritual-physical metaphoric being who gives herself to every lover who can give himself to her. But for this union the metaphysician would have to utter himself utterly, would have to pierce the voluminous cloaks and truly deal out his being indoors to the beloved. It is in such exchange of the simplest of speech, in such communication of the one common logos, that the weddings of the soul are consummated. But this merger of opposites, of the "I" and "thou," occurs not in the square rooms where metaphysicians plot their charts of reality, but in that arabesque domain where the in and out, the up and down are fused. The philosopher may work all the angles (Kant's herculean labor) but this serpentine realm will be permanently closed to him unless he puts off the complexities of matter and like the simplest of children sports upon the shore.[19] He must play by the dual light of the star on that ambiguous seacoast of "desert Florida" where man experiences himself as the dual creature of matter and spirit, as his own "thou" and "I."

> It is a good light, then, for those
> That know the ultimate Plato,
> Tranquillizing with this jewel
> The torments of confusion.

To hear the heavenly labials in a world of gutterals[20] is to know the spirit in the matter; and this is the goal of all men, of the poet as of the philosopher, but the philosopher is a man "without flash," [21] and without flesh. Such a goal is attained only by the dual flash of the charming emerald which is not the philosophers' stone, but the keystone of the poetic arch wherein is blended perfectly the yellow of matter and the blue of spirit, the yellow of the definite and the blue of the infinite. In this stone (which is the cornerstone of existence since it is the logos who contains all logoi, the unity who contains all multiplicity) we find the peace which passeth understanding, the pact which binds antinomies in a way which no metaphysician can comprehend.

The "ultimate Plato", then, has no more to do with historical Plato than the true man has to do with the mannikin. Like homunculus, historical Plato gives us only the ghostly paradigms of things, the mathematical model of reality, the gaunt fugitive phantom.[22] What ultimate Plato gives is the perfect merger of contradictories in the metaphors which are true: it is in his kingdom that the philosopher's "reason fades in the calmed twilight." [23] Beyond reason, beyond metaphysics (and beyond poetry, though Stevens could not see it) is that ultimate Plato who was a sign of chiasmus to the gentiles and in whom is the peace that passed even Stevens' conscious grasp.

This truly ultimate Plato remained for Stevens, as he was for the young Milton, only the *fabulator maximus*, only the composer of fictions in which we find brief consolation.[24] And it is this Plato (whom we must recognize then as only the "penultimate" Plato) who presides over one of the major poems in which poetry and philosophy are seen not in rivalry but as twin voices of the same despair. In this poem as in so much of Stevens' opus, there are no answers: man is only an animal compelled to choose between one absurdity and another—or at least so the poet explicitly affirms. (One emphasizes "explicitly" because even total despair at the absence of meaning hints at meaning somewhere.) [25]

"Asides on the Oboe" is exactly that, an "aside": rather than the firm and vigorous conviction of the believing poet. This oboe speaks in the muted accents of the unbelievable but insinuating temptation which gradually emerges even into the poet's imagination and finally takes possession of his person. This haut-bois, then, is not the high and sacred wood of Arcadia where men meet gods, but the *selva oscura*, the forests of the night where man loses himself in darkness.

> The prologues are over. It is a question, now,
> Of final belief. So, say that final belief
> Must be in a fiction. It is time to choose.

This is bravely stoic coinage; but as the poem advances, this heroically empty gesture provides only counterfeit solace.

> That obsolete fiction of the wide river in
> An empty land; the gods that Boucher killed;
> And the metal heroes that time granulates—
> The philosophers' man alone still walks in dew
> Still by the sea-side mutters milky lines
> Concerning an immaculate imagery.
> If you say on the hautboy man is not enough
> Can never stand as god, is ever wrong
> In the end, however naked, tall, there is still
> The impossible possible philosophers' man,
> The man who has had the time to think enough
> The central man, the human globe, responsive
> As a mirror with a voice, the man of glass,
> Who in a million diamonds sums us up.

Throughout the Western tradition from the Old Testament on, there have been three dominant modes—one might even say "styles"—for resolving man's mysterious relation with the universe: prophecy, priestcraft, kingship. All are here described as having failed: the gods are dead, the pantheons have been plundered by unsuccessful artists, and the tin soldiery of royalty has rusted out. Only the metaphysician still demands to be taken seriously;" he alone still claims to be signed with the chrism that imparts the power of fusing the divided image. The "dew upon their feet shall manifest" [27] the philosophers' anointing: the dew which washes the "dusk with silver," [28] transforms the chaotic into the ordered, and buds forth the savior who shall restore man to the garden state[29]—or so the metaphysician still claims. By the sea-side where the two worlds meet, the metaphysician continues his attempts to cloudily trace the world of spirit in matter; he continues to dwell in his own kind of Platonic twilight and his mutterings (like those long ago made by Jove the "muttering king") [30] make his own kind of "sweet moan." Unlike the defeated poets, he remains convinced that some day, if only he can think enough, he will be able to take this mimic world and join it to its pure principle, take this imagery and fuse it to the immaculate idea. But regrettably of all this he only talks: nothing happens. His mutterings never quite blend in that possible impossible union of logoi and logos which would not be muttering but uttering, which would be the absolutely unmuted utterance of the utterly utter—who is the God that no metaphysics encompasses. If the seductive voice of despair says that no one can ever truly join the world of unity and multiplicity (utterly utter himself) that no one can reach from end to end fusing this real world perfectly with the ideal world, the metaphysician says, wait, give me time, and you shall see these milky lines become the pure chiaroscuro which neither outlines nor defines but which conjoins and conducts.

But what in the end does the metaphysician supply? Only himself, only the human puzzle in a different calculus, and a calculus immeasurably more alien than that of the poet, for the poet, unlike the philosopher, doesn't merely pink and pink the ice-hard mass, he truly shapes it by jarring it, so that the wilderness where we dwell is no longer wild—it seems. All reality takes on the form of his ordering jar.[31] This jar contains all things—it seems—and therefore contents us. But then in this moment of supreme achievement—it seems—in this moment, the poet realizes he has made only another supreme fiction; even the poem fails, for "in contentment I still feel/ The need of some imperishable bliss."[32] The poet who jarred all reality so that the chaos took the form of his jar (*round* on the *ground* it sur*rounds*) has to admit in the end that he "cannot bring a world quite round."[33]

The poet works by negation, by travelling the apophatic way on the side of the seven storey mountain; but the metaphysician works by affirmation, by the kataphatic way on the plains of matter. The poet compresses all (apophasis) from alpha to omega into his jar; the metaphysician breaks the jar and seeks to add (kataphasis) the particles together: in a million diamonds to sum them up. But this common denominator of man is not a human being, is not the human metaphor, but only a human globe which is no more responsive or responsible than a mirror with a voice, and which does not join "this thing and that," but only reflects them. Because the poet is the image of the ideal man of ultimate Plato, and because the metaphysician is only the image of the poet, the metaphysician is always twice removed from perfection.[34] (In this lies the meaning of the title to the poem: the poet "*says*" on the haut bois in a close approximation of the simple speech of the logos, whereas the metaphysician can only offer "asides.") And it is precisely because the metaphysician never experiences as deeply as the poet the excruciating tension of these antipodes that he is so convinced that "given time"—as if this could happen in time—he will be able to fuse them perfectly.

125

There are only two dominant philosophical schools: the realist and the idealist. Stevens' perfect metaphysician, but imperfect man, naturally adheres to both:

> He is the transparence of the place in which
> He is, and in his poems we find peace.
> He sets this peddler's pie and cries in summer,
> The glass man, cold and numbered, dewily cries,
> "Thou art not August unless I make thee so."
> Clandestine steps upon imagined stairs
> Climb through the night, because his cuckoos call.

He is at once the Aristotelian microcosm and the Kantian *a priori*. The created really-out-there-now world is existent in him, or he creates the world that doesn't exist out there at all. Of the two options the Aristotelian appears to be favored—in its poems we find peace—while the Kantian is mocked for its incipient fascism: the metaphysician *sets* the clock of time ("Time, you old gypsy man") and almost like a poet cries out that it shall run backwards and fetch the age of gold, the august age. What catatonic tics, what ringings in the ears of metaphysicians begot the intricately elaborated systems that seek to bridge the world of light and darkness—this we are never told; we are told only that "Clandestine steps upon imagined stairs/ Climb through the night, because his cuckoos call."

But the summer of metaphysicians, the august age, even as the spring of poets, does not last:

> One year, death and war prevented the jasmine scent
> And the jasmine islands were bloody martyrdoms.
> How was it then with the central man? Did we
> Find peace? We found the sum of men. We found,
> If we found the central evil, the central good.
> We buried the fallen without jasmine crowns.
> There was nothing he did not suffer, no; nor we.

126

In this moment when things fall apart, when the center cannot hold, all the metaphysical mirrors are cracked. The philosopher isolate in the islands of the climbing plants where his *stairs* (the word-play is again on the voyeur, trapped in the world of *Anschbauung*, who only *stares*: "Look at the lavender/ And look your last and look still steadily....") climb through the night, cannot really give us the ladder of Jacob that joins heaven and earth; his "grades of being" never reach as "high as that." [35] Because the metaphysician in his se-curity and pride believes himself the successor of all ancient priests, poets, and kings (successor of "the gods that Boucher killed and the metal heroes") he arrogantly takes possession of the gardens where grow the flower that decked the catafalque of the priest-poet, King: "The tufted crow-tow, and pale jessamine/ ... strew the Laureate Hearse where Lycid lies." [36]

But like priest, prophet, and king before him, the philosopher cannot make the pact that signifies the joining of contradictories. In the last great breakdown we find no peace, we find only the same old dilemma again in its distilled form: we find "the central evil, the central good," and we find them in exactly that order. We do not have the paradoxic fusing of the central evil *and* the central good, but only on the one hand, the "central evil," and on the other hand, "the central good." The clasping of those hands in the Jeru-salem of metaphysics never takes place. [37] We remain abandoned in the same state of division: the evil and the good, the chaos and the order, the tiger and the lamb remain apart.

The bond, then, between poet and philosopher seems to be only that of table-mates at a banquet of ashes.

> It was not as if the jasmine ever returned.
> But we and the diamond globe at last were one.

127

> We had always been partly one. It was as we came
> To see him, that we were wholly one, as we heard
> Him chanting for those buried in their blood,
> In the forests that had been jasmine, that we knew
> The glass man, without external reference.

Metaphysician and poet had always been companions, if not intimates; but now they are plighted in their sweetest, saddest plight. For they recognize themselves as both driven to one seemingly meaningless destiny: chanting in the forests that had been jasmine. But—though Stevens does not say it—the old cycle must inevitably begin again: in the reversion to barbarism, the philosophers shall become the new prophets, priests, and kings, and the jasmine gardens will flourish in the new forests of the night. Stevens, thus, concludes his poem—if it can be said to be concluded—with a kind of affirmative negation. For, if there is absolutely no meaning, why chant at all? Why not, simply "all the rest is silence"? Because hope springs eternal? Not quite; but because: "Thee chantress oft the Woods among,/ I woo to hear thy even-song."[38] Because man is defined as a chanting animal enslaved to the wooing of peace, to the "performing" of the song that demands the full symphony in which all manner of things shall be one, in which every valley shall be exalted and every mountain and hill made low through the song of "even." Though there is no salvation, Stevens explicitly affirms, though there is no external reference by which man can have meaning, yet in his incantation over the mystery of being, he can find a link with his fellow and a moment of enchantment: "Supple and turbulent, a ring of men/ Shall chant in orgy on a summer morn/ . . . They shall know well the heavenly fellowship/ Of men that perish and of summer morn."[39] This chanting in the forests (*diese Toene* of Beethoven) implies as the poet-priest said that we "shall be made Thy music," the music which *"binden wieder,/Was die Mode streng geteilt."*[40]

For if there is no solution *whatever*, why chant at all? It is a question that cannot be answered by any poet as poet, and it is not even expressedly posed by Stevens. But *by the very fact of* positing this necessity for incantation, he points to the answer.[41]

> ... if there are conditioned beings, there also is the fulfilling of their conditions; and if there are no mere matters of fact that remain ultimately unexplained, then no conditions are fulfilled simply at random; all are fulfilled in accord with some exemplar; and so there must be an exemplary cause that can ground the intelligibility of the pattern in which are or would be fulfilled all conditions that are or would be fulfilled.

Or to say the same differently:[42]

> ... all the movement of our mind is only a long pursuit of the always fleeting intuition *of this Being.* Now the fundamental tendency of a faculty is indeed—if the notion of finality is to retain any meaning—the sign, at the very least, of a certain latent potentiality in that faculty. On the other hand, the human understanding, shut up in the narrow circle of the sensible and quantitative datum, does not in spite of all its efforts after synthesis and co-ordination, meet there its proper intuition. What are we to conclude from this, if not that our understanding—orientated in its most intimate foundation toward an 'intellectual intuition,' if such there be, that of pure Being—is not totally disproportioned to this kind of intuition, but that, on the other hand, the actual law of its exercise, imposing on it exclusively sensible 'presentations,' radically prevents it from making its acts equal this its deepest tendency? The antinomy of this fundamental attitude, this *desiderium naturale,* and the insurmountable restrictions which *intellectio in phantasmate* opposes to it, can only be removed by the intervention of an external force, capable of putting aside these restrictions by *directly* presenting to the

understanding its true object, Being. It is the final solution which the Christian religion proposes, by assigning as term to the action of man, aided by grace, the *very vision of God.*

By which I here understand to be meant that the very act of making song, however incomplete, and precisely because incomplete, implies the existence of the full diapason in another world, implies the aria of what Blake calls "the sweet round mouths."[43] We can, then, know nothing "without external reference," for this external reference is the Logos who re-fers-up-holds, and referees all things.

# 4

## The Dawn of the Sacred

It has become almost a commonplace of art criticism to affirm that we are experiencing in our time a development of art forms which have all the characteristics of the sacred art of the past: these forms are often non-representational, non-rational though highly intellectual, hieratic, and abstract. If the definition of these qualities seems to place an unwarranted emphasis on the negative, this is not surprising; for the sacred is to be defined to a great extent by its sense of separation and segregation, since it shares not only in the affirmative way of religious philosophers, but in the *via negativa* of the mystics.

Yet paradoxically this art of our time with its sacral traits remains an art dedicated to the exploitation of the world of the profane, of that world beyond the wall of the temple. And it is the resulting conflict within the artist, responsive to an innate passion for the sacred while orienting his work towards profane ends, that accounts, perhaps, both for the frustration and the agony embodied in much contemporary work which seems tormented by a kind of schizoid malaise, and also for the hesitant and almost covert manner in which the great exponents of sacred forms—one thinks of Picasso, Masson, or even of Pollock—introduce the images of the world of spirit, of the world of the temple, into their art; moreover, while shunning the notion of an infinite absolute, these artists seem to strive after a sort of impossible numerical infinity in the incessant repetition of themes and figures drawn from the realm of the myth. They appear, in fact, haunted by the sacred, while tormented by their own refusal to embrace an absolute which would allow complete freedom to this holy daimon within them.

Considering, then, this sacral character in modern art, though without ignoring its apparent dedication to profane ends, one may feel justified in anticipating for our age a renaissance without historic parallel of all the religious arts. The expectation of this renewal in the religious arts— that is, of the arts employing the traditional language of the sacred, and directed towards the work of the temple— is based not merely on the assumption that modern man, as eminent thinkers have reminded us, is in search of a soul, but rather on that necessary metaphysical law which states that a number of accidental mutations predisposes to substantial change. Given the gradual purification of the arts beginning with the romantic rebellion against the academy, progressing through the achievement of Cézanne who rejected mere sensation in his vision of a deeper architectural form, up to the astringently purifying experiments of the revolutionary artists of this century, it is manifest that the twilight and the dark night of the absolute have faded into a new dawn.

One might further suggest that the absence of this sense of the absolute from the art of the last three centuries represents a type of spiritual aridity, a type of vastation, similar to that of which the mystics have written, and that the lustral mission of Cézanne and his successors has constituted a saving ascesis for the modern spirit; it is through this asceticism that the prince of darkness, the tutelary spirit of Malraux' twilight, has been exorcised, and that the morning vision of the angels has become resurgent. Like many ascetic exercises, this one, too, has been subject to abuse; and, without extending the parallel too far, one might think of the Futurists as resembling certain flagellant sects, or of Mondrian as comparable to the followers of Scaramelli who, in the pursuit of asceticism as an end in itself, became lost in the "negative space."

It is in the theological notion of such a "matutinal vision" that we recognize the true meaning of an art of the sacred: it is an art totally dedicated to the work of the temple, and capable of offering an insight into that life of the absolute which a mere intellectual representation cannot provide. Such an art, as Father C. J. Dumont has said of the ikon, "conducts us to a reality inaccessible by any other approach." [1] Furthermore with regard to Christian art—which is *the* sacred art pre-eminently—it is a reflection of the life of the Trinity through Christ, who is envisioned not only as the eternal Logos, but as the God-man in all his theandric splendor.

The importance of a comprehensive theological synthesis is here evident. For a theology which contemns human nature, or which disdains the humanity of Christ, or which overlooks the imperfection of analogical knowledge in an arid crystallizing and mechanical categorizing of the divine life can never nourish a genuine religious art. Each of these three tendencies—as represented, for example, by the anthropology of the Flemish mystics as opposed to the incarnational tradition of the Fathers and St. Thomas, or by the mystical doctrine of the French School of spirituality as opposed to that of St. Teresa, or by the theological manuals of Tanquerey as opposed to the works of Scheeben—constitutes a theological divergency with obviously unfortunate repercussions in the artistic sphere; moreover, in each case it is not so much a question of unorthodoxy, as of a failure to accept fully the fact that Christ's humanity, and consequently all mankind, is more fully human because of the hypostatic union, and that our demeanor, our intellectual comportment, before this mystery is not that of a probing analyst, but of a reverent and awed worshipper.

This influence of a theological system on the religious arts is evident whether one considers stylistically the monophysite roots of iconoclasm, or thematically, the sacramental rather than sacrificial notions of the Eucharist in the van Eyck altarpiece and Raphael's Disputà. Relevant to our time, both the art *sulpicien* and that of Barclay Street can be seen as the expression of limited theological perspectives. In the case of the art of St. Sulpice, one encounters a reaction against the stern anti-humanism of the French School of spirituality, a reaction which took the form, first, of an excessive emphasis on whatever was richly sentimental, and second—as an orthodox counter-weight to Bérullian piety— of the popular cult of the Sacred Heart. This explains the enthusiasm for that devotion and the multiplication of its images among a people unconsciously thirsting for the re-assertion of an incarnational humanism; while it also indicates that in this slight temporary suspension of one of the lesser functions of the *ecclesia docens*, it was the Christian community which felt the need for a less negative spirituality, and which spontaneously fostered the development of the doctrinal apostolate of John Eudes and Claude de La Colombière.

A similar historical process is responsible for the art of Barclay Street. Catholic piety during the nineteenth century in this country as in Ireland was also anti-humanist and, Newman testifies, anti-intellectual; for there was a real bond between St. Sulpice and Maynooth, and between Bérullian severity and Irish rigorism. This anti-humanism flourished in the climate of liturgical apathy prevalent throughout the American Church, and led inevitably to the proliferation of private devotions, the sentimental character of which was the necessary consequence of a people starved emotionally on the religious plane and also—resulting from their isolation and poverty as immigrants—on the social. Deprived of the restrained exercise of the spiritual faculties in liturgical worship, the people sought such an exercise in private religious practices and in the relatively uncontrolled cultivation of devotional images without intellectual or doctrinal basis (e.g., the depiction of the Sacred Heart apart from the Sacred Humanity of Christ).

It is no mere coincidence, then, that all of the divergencies which I have mentioned came into being during periods when corporate participation in the eucharistic sacrifice had declined and individualistic piety was rampant. There is a reciprocal causality between the state of liturgical worship and the state of the religious arts, a reciprocity which is seen in recent Church history, for example, in the relation between the *Génie du Christianisme* and the restoration of Solesmes, or more significantly, in the relation between Ildefons Herwegen's *Art-principle of the Liturgy* and the liturgical revival of this century. "This essay," wrote Father William Busch in the preface to his translation of Abbot Herwegen's work, "unconsciously and unintentionally gave the first impulse to the Liturgical Apostolate in Germany in the year 1912."¹ Now it is this liturgical renaissance in its encounter with the sacral traits of contemporary art discussed above which accounts for the recrudescence of all the religious arts in our time.

Consequently, there is no exaggeration in asserting that the main reason why contemporary works are rejected by the majority of the Christian community is the failure of these works to rise out of the daily lives of the people. Moreover, the compulsory imposition of such works on the community will generally prove fruitless, for there is a

135

danger in striving along paths too direct to educate any-one esthetically. The multiplication of art works of the highest worth will alone rarely modify the general ethos. The community itself must be brought to see the need for a hieratic, genuine, objective religious art, an art which is an expression of liturgical life; and it can come to appreciate such an art only inasmuch as the people themselves are consciously aware of the serene and lucid objectivity of the Roman liturgy.

This is why art projects such as that sponsored in this country in 1949 by the Liturgical Arts Society and those sponsored at Assy and Audincourt in France, while they did much to introduce religious themes to the masters of contemporary art, and while they are intrinsically of great value, had less educative effect on the totality of the Christian people than the establishing of, let us say, the Missa recitata—which is not necessarily the ideal in corporate worship—in the most insignificant parish church. And this is also why it has been the religious communities both in this country and in Europe which have been the most ardent exponents of the modern idiom (one thinks of the French Dominicans or of the American Benedictines of St. John's Abbey), for it is they which are most firmly attached to the dogmatic and liturgical tradition.

Although the primary work in the current renaissance of the religious arts must be the task of those who by office or ordination have as their mission the religious formation of the Christian people, there nevertheless remains the important duty incumbent on artists and critics of defining more clearly the place of contemporary art in the church. Furthermore, if the notion of reciprocal causality mentioned above has any validity, then this duty parallels and is concomitant with the more generalized formative work.

In addition to the general culture of the person, two

136

specifics seem imperative here: first, the inculcation of an awareness of mystery in the presence of the great epiphanies of the human spirit: an inculcation which will demand a greater stress on the development of *sense*, and a consequent de-emphasis on that siccative and surgical analysis of art works which so often passes for explication. There is, according to Theodor Haecker's expression, "a metaphysic of feeling," and such a metaphysic would dictate an attitude of love and awe before the art work, rather than a conduct resembling systematic rape.[3]

Second, it is important that educators develop both in the plastic arts and in literature an appreciation of the place of symbolism. Such a development should not require instruction in the verbal significance of symbols, but rather would be concerned with conditioning the mind so that it did not reject the very need for such expression; this would be done on the basis of St. Thomas' principle that "similitudes drawn from things farthest away from God form within us a truer estimate that God is above whatever we may think or say."[4]

Turning, then, to a consideration of the actual place of the contemporary arts in the service of the altar, one is faced immediately with a number of problems, the first and most important of which is that of definition.[5] Traditionally the mission of religious art has been to minister to the instruction of the faithful. If its main task is to give a visual teaching of Catholic doctrine, as the late Msgr. Chevrot asserted,[6] then one might conclude, since faith is not a prerequisite for a rational presentation of Catholic teaching, that any artist of any or no religious belief may be commissioned in the work of the Church. If, however, one maintains that this catechetic role of the arts was to a considerable degree the result of the illiteracy of an earlier

**137**

era, one may find their function for our age in the capacity they have to create within the church structure an atmosphere of holiness, or what might be termed a sacred environment.

But this second role—which I accept as primary—would imply that only Catholic artists, who would realize by connatural intuition those forms which best express the Christian vision, should be employed in the work of the Church. And, perhaps, other things being equal (since technique cannot dispense with piety), this would be true; yet because genius knows no confessional limitations, these other things quite simply are not equal.

Assuming, then, the right of any competent artist to employ his talents in a liturgical art, it nevertheless does not seem necessary to justify this right on the following assumption of the late Père Couturier:[7]

> We do not know what goes on in the innermost recesses of the heart—nor what spiritual deficiencies may be made up by the intuitions of genius. Genius does not give the faith, but there exists between mystical experience and that of the great heroes and artists a very profound analogy.

Such a line of reasoning on the part of Père Couturier—whom one criticizes only with the deepest esteem for his own great accomplishment—seems a bit tenuous; for no matter how profound an analogy may exist, it remains analogy: *simpliciter* different, *secundum quid* the same.

The defense which Père Couturier so valiantly sought, and which must be realized if there is to be established an acceptable rationale for permitting the pagan artist access to the Christian Church, can perhaps best be clarified on the grounds that any art work, whether by pagan or Christian, remains a natural thing functioning in a manner similar to the natural theology of Aristotle in relation to the Christian theology of Aquinas: it leads one to the foot of the altar; it does not, nor is it intended that it should, bring about a communion with the Presence there.[8]

Even in the case of an artist assumed to be "atheist," there is no justification for excluding his work from the church on religious grounds—though prudence might suggest reasons—for the art work is likened to a sacramental rather than to a sacrament: that is, it takes its Christian character not from the mere fact of its being "confected" and directed by the artist to liturgical ends, but from the prayer of the whole Church to whose service it is ordained when it is blessed or consecrated with the church building.

If all that has been said above assumes the ineluctable necessity and the Christian obligation in justice of employing the finest craftsmen regardless of religious affiliation, it also assumes implicitly that the motive for such employment is simply the glorifying of the Christian temple. Unfortunately when encountering certain ardent apologists of different modern tendencies, one sometimes has the impression that less noble ends are being pursued: some seem intent on proving that there can be no incompatibility between the ideals of the latest avant-garde cult and Catholicism; some are apparently merely seduced by each new fluctuation of the Zeitgeist; while others, through a misguided zeal for souls, seem to attenuate Christian principle and to ignore Christian sensibility so that their own personal apostolate in the modern world will succeed; more yet seem naively to attempt to establish the excellence of the present by the mediocrity of the past. There is prevalent a legitimate disgust for the sentimentality and archaism of much traditional popular religious art, so that when a work is achieved which is without these faults, its advent is often hailed with enthusiasm—the fact that one extreme may have replaced another is frequently overlooked.

139

There is no need for extending this catalogue, since it is pointless to carry on a discussion such as this with the assumption of bad faith on anyone's part. Yet, while the exact significance of Pius XII's condemnation of "monstrosities in certain arts which even pretend to call themselves Christian" cannot be determined exactly, it should be obvious that every pious project undertaken by well-meaning Catholics and employing the forms of the modern idiom is not necessarily deserving of unqualified praise. Such a statement as that of the late Holy Father is not, certainly, directed at any particular artist, and hence ought not to be applied to any; regrettably there have been those standing in the wings, eager to pounce on any papal phrase, who have not hesitated to particularize such pronouncements, and who have used them under the guise of a virtuous obedience to bludgeon any and all critics and artists who do not conform to their own peculiar and often paranoiac canons of taste—not surprisingly, the fuss such people raise is in inverse proportion to the wisdom and insight they display.

However, prescinding from the ordinary legitimate exercise of critical intelligence, there are examples of other condemnations of contemporary work which are in every way justifiable, and which may even be said to serve the cause of artistic progress. These are the expressions of the bishops when it is a matter of safeguarding for prudential or doctrinal reasons the faithful of their own dioceses against the occasional shocks which the distortion or the novelty of certain works may cause. Now, no one would claim that bishops are more highly endowed esthetically than the rest of mankind, but in virtue of their office, of their experience, and of their empathic awareness of the condition of the faithful, they have a right and a duty to interdict whatever may disturb their people unnecessarily.

Moreover, such interdiction will have over the years the beneficial result of obviating the danger of any extended reaction setting in permanently against the contemporary art forms.

Thus, the removal of Richier's crucifix from the chapel at Assy can be justified on prudential and doctrinal grounds, not on esthetic. Nevertheless the obligation of making a valid judgment in such cases demands that each art work be assessed individually, so that what may be considered imprudent in one diocese might be acceptable in another; and what would offend insular parochial standards might be a stimulus to reverent prayer in the clearer atmosphere of a university or monastic community.

Condemnations such as that of the Richier sculpture point up another area where some clarification is necessary: to what extent is the artist justified in distorting the body of Christ to conform to his own creative intuition? This problem, which seems to vex unduly those who never before took an interest in the religious arts, can be resolved only by an examination of the entire continuum of Christ-tian art. Down through the centuries every artist has portrayed the God-man according to the dictates of his own inspiration, yet it is obvious that the Christ of the catacombs differs from the Christ of Giotto, of Michel-angelo, of El Greco, or of Rouault.[9] The artist in every case is not to be regarded as using the body of Christ as merely a pretext for exploring new forms, or as merely a technical exercise; but rather he is to be seen as an imitator of the *supreme Artifex* who formed in the womb of the Virgin the body of the Son of man. Each artist's repre-sentation, then, is an attempt to "utter the good word" in a necessarily fragmentary and partial approximation of the heights and depths in him who was described as a worm and no man, and also as the most beautiful of the sons of man.

We are concerned in this problem with artistic objectives only; for, if the form given to the body of Christ—whether it be the accepted religious oleograph or the so-called Jansenist crucifix—has been guided exclusively by religious principles, it will be defective, not because of any possibly erroneous dogmatic conception, but by reason of its derivation from non-esthetic sources. Similarly, a pure work generated in the purest interiority, but judged unfit for liturgical use on prudential or doctrinal grounds, generally ought not to be modified to make it acceptable, for once the integrity of the original esthetic impulse is tampered with, the way is open to continuing abuse. And, historically, it will often be found that the artist, depending on his own sensibility and vision, has grasped the doctrinal significance more firmly than his critics who do not really *see* his work, and so reject it in the name of a spurious theological accuracy.[10]

The artist must, of course, rely on theological wisdom, but such a reliance should not be founded on an abstract knowledge of the Christian fact and its corollaries, since then the Christianity of the work will be constituted as merely an artificial and appliqué element. Instead there should be a gradual and organic assimilation of this theological wisdom so that it will be molded into the form of the work from the very moment of its inception. More precisely, then, there should be some direction on the part of theologians to clarify the relation of the art work to its liturgical setting. Such direction, it would seem, was overlooked in the execution of Jean Lurçat's tapestry at Assy which, rather than framing the altar to focus on the Eucharistic Sacrifice, tended to diffuse attention in a scattering of apocalyptic symbols.

However, should the artist himself hesitate to exploit certain themes, such a scruple should be respected. Not every artist can develop a crucifixion; nor every artist, a resurrection. And one would no more be justified in requiring of each individual artist such spiritual versatility than one would have been in expecting from Mr. T. S. Eliot a poem exalting industrial civilization—or human love.

There is certainly some danger that in the theological guidance of the artist one may so circumscribe him with rules and legalistic prescriptions that the force of his vision is blocked and cannot mature. In denial of this danger, a good deal of romantic ink has been spent to point out how medieval craftsmen frequently had dictated to them both the nature of the work to be done and detailed orders as to its execution. In reply to this one can only state—though various neo-medievalists will ignore it— that it is very likely the work suffered therefrom; in any event it ought to be allowable to ascribe the disappearance of such programmatic outlines to esthetic progress: progress which does not consist in embracing the accidentals while rejecting the substance of a tradition, nor in raising fourteenth-century barriers merely so that twentieth-century artists can hurdle them.

One may suggest, then, in the light of all these principles, that the basic directive for the liturgical arts ought to be summarized in a statement as simple and uncluttered as: whatever does not minister to the service of the altar and to its attendant rites and devotions is to be excluded. Defining a liturgical art as a "committed" and therefore "functional" art, one might sympathize with the viewpoint— though not necessarily with its application here—of the following letter written shortly after a glowing account of the chapel at Vence had appeared in the London *Tablet*: "Dear Sir.—Can your enthusiastic correspondent inform us whether the Dominicans have installed a lift to enable us to make our devotions before M. Matisse's perpendicular series of Stations of the Cross?—Yours faithfully, *Evelyn Waugh*." [11]

An even greater danger in any extra-esthetic direction, whether it be religious, social, or political, is that it tends to canonize certain styles as the only adequate expression of a particular thematic material. Especially is this so of priestly direction, as the history of art from the Egyptian to the Beuronese sadly testifies. Theologians who often must arrive at doctrinal formulae as exact as possible incline quite instinctively to carry over this passion for precision into other fields—in the case of the arts, the results are often only comparable to what one might have had if Cardinal Zigliara had ever attempted a translation of Mallarmé.

Yet it is not only theologians who may seek to define liturgical art in terms of a specific style; it is a tendency also of laymen and artists, as the following criticism of Eric Gill indicates: "Of the portion of the liturgical art movement that Gill leavened it may be similarly said: They rejoice at having replaced in their churches the neo-Gothic style by the pseudo-Byzantine." [12] Now there is no doubt that Gill's style, pure and firmly delicate as it was—save when it degenerated into mannerism in the hands of his followers—has been for good and bad reasons identified in the English-speaking world with "liturgical art." Such criticism would be welcome, then, were it not that its author, Jean Charlot, had developed a style which relies not on vertical elongations, but instead slings its forms along a horizontal plane, in direct antithesis to Gill's; and so one wonders whether Charlot would have been equally vocal had it been a question of replacing the neo-Gothic by what might be called "pseudo-Mayan." However, since there is no technique for liturgical art, one may certainly esteem

Charlot's religious work without repudiating that of Gill.

Furthermore—since there is no single style, whether ethical or ethnical—to speak of a "liturgical art movement," as if it involved a particular type of art, is to departmentalize excessively; for, in the case of Gill there was the affirmation of a way of life which flowed from the deepest fonts of natural instinct and evangelical faith, of that instinct and faith which Father Régamey so eloquently anatomizes in his book, *Religious Art in the Twentieth Century*. And I would add, in concluding, that Gill's example, while singular, offers one of the few illustrations in our time of that total engagement to an integral Christian humanism from which alone can come a spiritual, a moral, and an esthetic renaissance.

In this renaissance all styles as all men have a voice in singing the *new* canticle. And though each shall sing in his own tongue, all shall be understood in the one language of the arts celebrating the *magnalia Dei*.

145

# The Christian Themes of Marc Chagall

THIRTY-FIVE years ago, Oswald Spengler wrote: "What do we possess today as art? A faked music, filled with artificial noisiness of massed instruments; a faked painting, full of idiotic, exotic, and show card effects, that every ten years or so concocts out of the form-wealth of millennia some new 'style' which is in fact no style at all since everyone does as he pleases; a lying plastic that steals from Assyria, Egypt, and Mexico indifferently." [1] Whether one agrees that modern art is one of the signs of the great *Untergang*, it nevertheless is certain that it accurately mirrors the cultural turmoil of the first half of this century. But it is certain, too, that the new artistic orientation with its emphasis on the subconscious and the irrational, with its probing for the meaning of life, of reality, and of art itself, has directly or indirectly increased our knowledge of man.

Perhaps the outstanding criticism that can be brought to bear upon much twentieth-century creative work stems from its attempt to transcend its own plastic limitations. Contemporary artists tried to ape the metaphysician in penetrating reality, and they have, in a futile effort at a kind of inverse mysticism, sought to shape spirit with matter. Gris attempted to make a rhetoric of painting, while le Corbusier, when yet a painter, sought to convert it into an architecture, and the Futurists emulated the scientists with their stroboscopic effects. Similarly the modern movement was too self-consciously rebellious against the past, and failing to create a positive esthetic to replace what it had destroyed, often was forced instead to canonize certain styles as the ultimate in artistic perfection. For a painter to devote his work—if only theoretically—to the mission which Dali assigned himself of organizing "confusion and thus to help completely discredit the world of reality," [2] is to make a career of negations—a career which in its literal objectives verges on the diabolic. And there is in the bland faked neoclassicism of Dali's painting since the thirties a kind of photographic imitation of God's work which can best be described as diabolic, precisely because Dali so caricatures authentic creativity. Since so many contemporary artists, even those not directly attached to the Dada revolt, rejected almost entirely the heritage of the past, they were forced to create innumerable new styles and techniques, which with the exception of Picasso and Mondrian they frequently failed to exploit fully.

Yet just as out of the artistic fervor and confused experimentation of the Provençal love poets came the stylistic revolution of the *Divina Commedia,* so also from the creative turmoil of the modernist movement which begot such publications as *Blast, Élan,* and *Der Sturm* has come the candid purity—the sweet new style—of Marc Chagall's paintings. This innocent and childlike art of Chagall had to be born, like any other child, in passion and confusion, in suffering and anguish.

An artist of the stature and achievement of Marc Chagall could have been nurtured only on rebellion against those static, arid symbols which the revolutionary artists so violently opposed. Born as he was into an artistic world of stale and vapid signs, the clichés of two centuries of academicism, Chagall was forced to create with his contemporaries of the Fauve and Die Brücke movements a new vocabulary of symbolism. But this new language was to be for him more than it was for his fellow painters; as early as 1910 on his arrival in Paris he had spurned what he termed the "earthly conceptions" of the Fauvists and early cubists, and had begun his search for an idiom which would express the super-reality of this universe.

Thus he came to create that style which has been the confusion of so many critics: a style which expresses everything which is deepest in the traditions of the Jewish people. And it is perhaps because modern critics have failed to penetrate into the meaning of a specifically Jewish art that they have been so hasty in aligning Chagall to the surrealist school. For it is only when Chagall is seen in the light of his religious background that his creative significance emerges. Technically influenced by the surrealists and the Expressionists, what gives the work of Chagall its specific character is its perfect reflection of the spirit of the Diaspora Jews, the Jews of the little ghetto villages of Russia and Poland.

Just as we may explain that opulent contentment with life and actualité which suffuses the great religious paintings of the Catholic tradition only by seeing this spirit of satisfaction with the present in the light of the theology of the sacraments—for the sacrament actualizes and makes contemporary the historical Christian fact; and just as we may explain the somber pessimism of traditional Protestant art in the light of Lutheran and Calvinist theology, so too, it is only when we examine Chagall's theological tradition that we fully understand the unique qualities of his artistic message. For a Jewish artist, lacking the sacrament to make the past contemporary as has the Catholic artist, and lacking a central point in history for his doctrinal beliefs as has the Protestant artist, can look only to the future for the realization of his messianic hopes.

And this explains that pathos which penetrates all the religious paintings of Marc Chagall. There is evident in this art not that intense and highly articulate anguish which the existentialists of his own period in Paris anatomized, but rather the deep-down fermenting resignation of a people conscious of its sacred character and confident of its future deliverance. One encounters this pathos in the mysterious melancholy expressed by the dumb beasts pictured in so many of the paintings. In their mute resignation they stand as symbols of the "expectation of the creature who waiteth for the revelation of the sons of God." Similarly one can understand the meaning of the clocks and violins which are thrust so naively and with such simple abandonment into the midst of the most intensely religious paintings, as if to tell the observer that salvation for the Jews can come only *in time*. The clock which defines time, and music which is the art of time, represent little to Catholic theology, which sees salvation in the present—"*now* is the acceptable time"—or to traditional Protestant thought which, until Kierkegaard, conceived the salvific act to be past; but such symbolism means much to a faith which looks to a new "fullness of time" for salvation.

But while an awareness of the Jewish tradition is indispensable for an understanding of Chagall's work, one must not confuse that tradition with the nationalism expressed by contemporary Zionist painters. His art breathes the spirit not of any conquering lion of Judah, but rather the spirit of the Lamb of the New Testament. For what is notable is that Chagall in these paintings envisions Christianity and Judaism as one tradition. Without repudiating his Jewish character, and painting with a deep realization of his dignity as one of God's chosen people, he tends toward that

THE CHRISTIAN IMAGE

unity of viewpoint which one may hope will develop between the Jew of the Diaspora and the enlightened Christian. Indeed, in his first great religious painting, the crucifixion of 1938, he shows how the candelabra, which is his recurrent symbol of the Jewish faith, having been overturned before the synagogue, remains upright only at the foot of the cross. In a world of racist madness, he tells us, it is the Christian and the Christian Church that must defend the Jewish belief.

And as in all great art we have a chiaroscuro of happiness and sadness, so too in Chagall there is in addition to the deepest pathos an underlying note of innocent joy. This is the joy which Bella Chagall wrote of in *Burning Lights* with a candid clarity that paralleled the art of her husband's paintings. It is the innocent joy of biblical man before his nature was fractured by sin; it is the joy of Francis of Assisi when he sang of his "sister earth," or when he spoke to "Brother Wolf," and preached to the birds. And in this we see another explanation of those silent beasts in the paintings; for these animals are here in the world of innocence as they were in the Garden before the fall, the friends and companions of man. One can readily see, then, why Chagall delighted in illustrating the fables of La Fontaine in 1927; and one can understand why in the later paintings, Chagall has the mute beasts themselves bring to the crucified Christ their homage of sinless and untainted creation.

This delicate evocation of joy and pathos reminds one of Blake's *Songs of Innocence*; for the art of Chagall, wrought in the dream world of childhood, blends into a unity the sacred Jewish traditions which have echoed through the ages, and views them through the multi-dimensional mirror of ghetto life, of naive love for the domestic animals of the village, and of sympathy for the burdened musicians, beggars, and priests of his people. It almost seems that from the time of his marriage with Bella, Chagall's work acquired this new understanding and this new delight in the traditions of his race. There are in the paintings of this later period less of the Expressionist severity and harshness which was evident in the earlier studies of Vitebsk. The joy of his marriage seems to have overflowed into the paintings which, with their vaporous film of misty color, powdery and irridescent—perhaps an effort to depict the shadowy recollections of childhood—awaken a new vision of love and reverence for life. This period of simply accepting God's world, and of rejoicing in the mysteries which it unfolded was the necessary preparation for his more specifically religious work when the Nazi persecutions aroused Chagall from nostalgic reverie to a total committment of his art to the struggle for his people.

Yet even in those latter paintings, so pregnant with the artist's deepest conviction, there is none of that blatant didacticism which so disfigures the propaganda paintings of Russian and American art of this same period. Had Chagall not developed in his artistic growth through a period of naive wonderment and love for all created things, then it seems probable that he too, like his Jewish contemporary, Chaim Soutine, would have succumbed to an anguishing despair in the face of his inner confusion and the plight of his people. There is certainly little joy in these pictures, but neither is there anything of despair. They utter forth an act of deepest faith in the sanctifying mission of the crucified Christ. Whether this is an act of supernatural faith in a person rather than commitment to a symbolic figure can hardly be determined in a critical study such as this.

151

Turning now to a consideration of three of the major works in which Chagall has painted the crucified Christ and in which the dominant themes of all his religious paintings appear, one soon realizes—as when reading many contemporary poets—that while one may not always know the meaning of particular images or symbols, yet the total impact, the significance of the composite, is readily grasped.

In the *Crucifixion* of 1938—the first of the Nazi-era paintings of Christ—the image of the God-man is suspended over a world of rape and pillage. The dull gray which gives the tone to this universal scene of destruction is broken only by the shaft of light which unites the cross with the saints of the Old Law hovering, like Botticelli's angels, over the sacred landscape. On the left there is the carnage of the sporadic Soviet outbreaks against the Jews, while on the right one sees the burning and looting of the synagogue by the Hitler armies. Here the Torah is in flames and the holy vessels and the candelabra of the temple are overturned; only at the foot of the cross does the candle of Jewish faith burn upright radiating its eternal message: "Arise, be enlightened, O Jerusalem"; and here only at the foot of the cross is there refuge for the sacred writings and for the persecuted people who bear the insulting placards designating them as Jews. Certainly the Son of God who was born a son of Abraham looks down with compassion on this multitude of his own people so suffering and maltreated. In the ladder which is present in this work, as well as in the *Crucifixion* of 1943, there is, perhaps, a symbol of that ladder of Jacob—which appears in other paintings also—upon which the saints are to ascend to their happiness.

In the *Crucifixion en jaune* of 1943 we have a more explicit affirmation of the unity of the two testaments. In this

painting the Torah and the candle, symbolic of the Old
Law, are placed on an equal plane with the cross of Christ,
symbolic of the New Law, while the angel of both testaments trumpets the Gospel of these new "good tidings." In
the background the saints of traditional Jewish folklore,
the beggars and fish-peddlers, look down upon the destruction raging beneath them. And fleeing from this destruction is a young woman with her child. This is the first
time Chagall has painted the Virgin Mary. And he sees in
her flight into Egypt a symbol which in its cosmic reach
spans the ages and joins the expulsion of the Jews from
the Holy Land into Babylon with their flight before the
Nazi persecution. Thus Mary, true daughter of Sion, becomes with her divine Son the link between the two testaments.

In *Chute de l'Ange*, begun in 1923 and finally completed
in 1947, one encounters the familiar figures of the Torah
and the houses of Vitebsk. Here, too, are the violin and the
clock, recollections of the painter's childhood, but meaningful here as symbols of the Jewish longing for a salvation
which is yet to come; and present also is the head of one of
those plaintive beasts whose appearance in the paintings
we have discussed above. In this work, the Virgin Mary
is seen not in the guise of her flight into Egypt, but as the
Mother of God of traditional hagiography. There is a
serenity about *The Fall* which the paintings of the period
of antisemitic persecution do not possess. Perhaps the long
penance which the Jewish people underwent at the hands
of the German government won for them that peace which
is to be found only in the cross. In any case, the candle
which burns so calmly at the foot of the cross recalls the
words of the last of the Jewish prophets: "Be mindful from
whence thou art fallen ... or else I come to thee, and will

153

move thy candlestick out of its place, except thou do penance." Certainly the presence of the fallen angel seems to have been on the part of Chagall a premonition of the violent persecution which his people were to undergo—a persecution which would draw them nearer to the cross, and which would be for them a means of filling up that which is lacking in the passion of their God.

There is only one figure, besides that of Christ, which appears in each of these paintings: that of a bent old man, cane in hand, carrying on his back a moth-eaten sack. From Chagall's *My Life*[3] we learn that this old beggar is an image of Elias; and as Elias fled from the wrath of Achab so has the wandering Jew fled through the ages from the recurrent persecutions of his enemies. Because it is the temporal destiny of the chosen people to wander over the earth until they arrive at the New Jerusalem, the Church of the Messiah, the cane carried by the traveling beggar has a significance relative to the staves carried during the Passover meal: "... with sandals on your feet and your staff in your hand ... like those who are in flight." This old man, present in all of these paintings, bespeaks the perpetual exodus which has been the fate of the Jews.

It is difficult to determine how extensively one may carry such explication of the paintings, but it is obvious that any art work transcends the terms of the artist's objective intention and takes on a deeper meaning from historical or psychological analysis. Thus Chagall's use of human heads on animal bodies, which has been explained factually as simply a blending of scenes from village life, may be more readily understood, in the light of the clarification that I am attempting here, as the result of a true primitive's vision—a child's vision—of the union between man and nature.

Similarly in much of Chagall's work one cannot but be

154

struck by the distortion of the human face which is sometimes reversed to look backwards, sometimes is blinded, or
sometimes has features facing both forward and backwards.
Surely there is something deeper in the meaning of these
images than simply their shock value; although Chagall himself believed that to be their major function in the paintings. We are justified, I feel, in seeking a more truly universal value in such figures. Thus we might see in the
human face which looks in two directions at once a kind
of archetypal symbol of Israel, who stands at the center of
history: an eternal people, looking to the past and to the future. And perhaps one might also regard these blind or
partly blinded figures as in some way expressive of a lack
of fullness in the traditional Hebrew world-picture. There
seems to be in them some suggestion of that eschatological
longing which is evident in the pathetic and heroic life of
Simone Weil who apparently in her *attente de Dieu* was
unable to remove from the eyes of her heart the scales of
indecision. The painter is here touching upon the Christian
tradition in art which from the fourteenth century has depicted the Old Testament as a maiden blindfolded. But he
is above all acknowledging with the entire biblical tradition—whether Old or New Testament—that to *know* God
is simply to *hear* his voice. These touching sightless faces
in Chagall's work seem to say with the blind Trophaea in
Gertrud von Le Fort's *Papst aus dem Ghetto:* "Why am I
here? Tell me, why am I here? I can see nothing." And
the Jewish heroine in Claudel's *Père Humilié* exclaims: "I
see no stars. I can only stand and listen. I can't see, I can
only hear."

And Israel, too, in the paintings of Marc Chagall is blind
and is a maiden. This feminine element in the genius of
the Jewish people explains why the artist can sketch the

155

male torso—as he does in *Via Dolorosa*—with the breasts of a woman. In Chagall's paintings of men with the forms of women there is the same syncretic blending that we meet with throughout the Bible, and which is best illustrated in these two texts: "No longer shall you be called Jacob, but Israel shall be your name. Thus God named him Israel" (Genesis 35: 10); "And the Lord said: Hast thou seen what rebellious Israel hath done? *She* hath gone of herself upon every high mountain..." (Jeremias 3:6). Only by fusing the male and female forms could Chagall express in his paintings the unique mission of the Jews as the warrior nation defending the divine covenant and as the bride of Yahweh.

The intellectual game of drawing literary and artistic parallels, having been abused in so much nineteenth-century criticism, has undergone a rather considerable eclipse in recent years. Yet such comparisons, if not overextended, do serve their purpose in placing a given artist in proper relation to the continuum. Thus one might think of paralleling the vibrancy of the Berlioz *Requiem* with the startling theatrical effects of a Caravaggio, or of linking the imperturbable placidity of Vermeer of Delft with the restrained piety of Schütz, or of comparing the stridency of Rossini's Mass *Solennel* with the florid intensity of de la Tour's religious paintings. And one thinks, perhaps, of seeing in the poetry and music of Chagall's period some parallel to his own religious sensibility; but the uniqueness of Chagall's achievement was to rise from the age of surrealism without succumbing to the techniques of that school. Even Max Jacob who could write:

Le Christ est mon bien

Je ne dis plus rien

or Apollinaire who declared in *Zone: Seul en Europe tu n'es pas antique ô Christianisme*—both of these contemporaries who were close to Chagall reflect a completely different spirit in their art.

Technically the art of Chagall makes one hark back to the age of the great contrapuntalists, to that age which perfected the art of the fugue. In listening to the *Incarnatus est* of Bach's *Mass in B* one can appreciate most fully both the spirit and the technique which are reflected in the work of Marc Chagall. Here one feels that interplay of themes surrounding the melody of Christ bringing to men the law of love. Rarely in figured music is the transcendent meaning of the Incarnation brought out so fully as in this Bach passage where the pure air hovers throbbingly and surgingly over a humanity torn by anguish and discontent. And this is the God Chagall depicts, a God transcendent, as one would expect any Jewish painter to envision him, and yet a God who places himself in the midst of his creatures. There is present throughout these religious paintings of Chagall that delicate network of themes, the candelabra, the Torah, the village, the innocent beasts, groaning and travailing, while the one dominant melody of the redeeming Christ, suspended above this universe of childlike vision and frightening strife, draws all things unto himself.

Among the poets, one thinks of certain themes in the work of Rainer Maria Rilke as comparable to those in the art of Marc Chagall. For Rilke, too, believed in a God transcendent and remote from the world of man: a God compounded out of all the most awesome traits described in the Old Testament and who objectified the poet's personal pessimism and a theological heritage which could find no place for the analogy of being. Yet it was Rilke

who in the *Marien-Leben* paid tribute to the Virgin Mary
and who wrote of her Son:

> Sieh, der Gott, der über Völkern grollte,
> macht sich mild und kommt in dir zur Welt.

Themes such as this well illustrate the religious background
and the underlying motif of Marc Chagall's work.

Writing as an American one is inclined to wonder what
should be the impact of an artist of Chagall's stature on that
American culture which he himself so much admired. Any
such estimate is, of course, contingent on one's larger attitude toward this culture. In general it seems that without
succumbing to any declension theories we yet may maintain that our culture, in its public and social strata, has
inclined toward material goods rather than to spiritual
values; and we might maintain further that this inclination
has been accelerated to an alarming degree by the three
wars. Given two generations that have had their idealism
cramped and thwarted, what can any painter who is ad-
hering to a spiritual tradition have to say?

It is necessary to preface our question as to the meaning
of an artist like Chagall to our country and our time with
the above remarks, for if he has no meaning, no deeply
spiritual meaning, then we might well accuse him—as Jean
Charlot has accused the majority of contemporary painters
—of neglecting the larger themes of man's plight while
pursuing self-analysis and pictorial technique.

Chagall's art, then, faces the culture of our people as
the innocent eyes of a child would face the cold gaze of
a confirmed and indifferent sinner. And as Bernanos and
Dostoevsky have so often shown, just as the confirmed sinner might be unmoved before an adult of mature and well-
disciplined spirituality, yet he would be touched to tears by

the poignancy of the naively upturned face and expectant glance of an innocent child. While other painters affect us by their psychological acuity or their intellectual penetration, Chagall moves us—and more specifically would move the man of our age and our country—by his serene innocence. Here we have not the heroic virtue of the saint who has sought the vision of truth by self-mastery and a rigorous asceticism; rather we have here a virtue which seems never to have been even remotely seared by the brand of personal sin.

Other painters may be extolled for their technical brilliance, for their mastery of their subject, or for their manual dexterity; but these qualities—no matter how evident—are not what we praise in Chagall. In Chagall one finds an art reminiscent of the great primitives, of that body of Franciscan painters who were afflicted with the *man' che trema* because they were so overwhelmed by the vision of the universe their faith opened to them. One feels that the technical defects for which Chagall has been so severely criticized result not from any artistic flaw, but simply from his realization of the cosmic import and significance of his vision: a vision which embraces the *Deus tremendus* of the Old Law and the *Deus fascinans* of the New. When speaking of the ineffable one can only mumble: when painting the invisible and intangible, the trembling hand is merely a proof of the authenticity of the artist's vision.

Such was the vision of Giotto and the vision of Fra Angelico; it is the vision of those who see that Christ came, as he said, not to destroy the Law and the prophets, but to fulfill them. This is not the world of religious passion—the world of El Greco—nor the world of religious emotion—the world of de Morales—nor the world of religious agony—the world of Valdés Leal. The world of Marc Chagall is the world of innocent man who has clouded the image of God within him by his blindness, by his stumbling, and by his cowardice. But more than this it is the world where God in that infinite sympathy for his creatures, which is the Incarnation, compassionates man and his weaknesses.

# NOTES

## I: The Word and the Words

1. "The little dog laughed to see such sport" because he was the dog "that's friend to man" ("The Waste Land," 74), and whose star when unveiled fructifies the tree of the one and the many of which the clumsy lust-play of Sweeney is only the carnal parallel ("Sweeney Among the Nightingales," 9-12):

> Gloomy Orion and the Dog
> Are veiled; and hushed the shrunken seas;
> The person in the Spanish cape
> Tries to sit on Sweeney's knees.

2. The number ten is both symbol and figure of the union of the one and the many. As symbol: unity plus multiplicity, that is, one plus three leads back to the original unity, back to one and zero: $1+3+3+3=10$. As figure: in Roman numerals the fusion of the one and the many is depicted in the sign of the chiasm, X; in Arabic numerals 1 & 0 is the sign of the lance and the chalice, as well as of the tree and the fountain: 9. This is why the poet "who sees into the life of things" ("Tintern Abbey," 48) places his all-ordering "jar in Ten-nessee" ("Anecdote of the Jar," 1).

3. See my reflections on "Why Ought Implies Can," in *Review of Metaphysics*, June, 1963.

4. 5:32.

5. "The Sense of the Sleight-of-hand Man," 2.

6. "To What Serves Mortal Beauty?" 4-5.

7. Psalm 44: 2; translated in the *Bible de Jérusalem*, "A beautiful poem has welled up from my heart."

8. Thus St. Thomas, "*Bonum rationem entis includit*," *De Veritate*, 21, 2.

9. It is this unity and simplicity that Milton is seeking to communicate when he has God the Father speak in the plainest and most repetitious language—all in sharp contrast to the rich diction of the Son or the angelic host and above all, of Satan. As Wallace Stevens says of the metaphysician,

> The innermost good of their seeking
> Might come in the simplest of speech.

But it is not only philosophy and metaphysics which is tautology as Kierkegaard said; it is everything. Everything is the tautology of the Logos, the multiple echo of the one word.

10. "On the Morning of Christ's Nativity," 14.

11. Respectively: "Ode to a Nightingale," 52, and "Jesu," 9.

12. "Les lettres du voyant," to George Izambard and to Paul Demeny.

13. "What I Do Is Me," 5-8:

> Each mortal thing does one thing and the same:
> Deals out that being indoors each one dwells;
> Selves—goes itself: myself it speaks and spells,
> Crying *What I do is me:* for that I came.

14. "His speech was with power," Luke 5: 32.

15. *Nullam obicem ponere* is the classic formula for the requirements of fit reception of the sacraments, and signifies here simply an openness to being.

16. It is a definition of poetry that Blake is offering in "Evening Star," 9-10:

> Speak silence with thy glimmering eyes
> And wash the dusk with silver.

And so too, Milton in "Il Penseroso," 55:

> And the mute silence hist along.

17. "The Candle Indoors," 12; the immediate reference is, of course, to Matthew 7:3.

18. "O admirabile commercium! Creator generis humani animatum corpus sumens. . . ." Antiphon for first vespers in the Roman liturgy, January first.
19. "Il Penseroso," 37-40.
20. St. Paul's statement on ". . . the Father of our Lord Jesus Christ of whom all paternity on heaven and earth is named" (Ephesians 3:15) is the ground of analogy whereby we apply to the finite those perfections which are pre-eminently in the infinite.
21. "The Ecstasy," 73-76:

> And if some lover such as we,
> Have heard this dialogue of one,
> Let him still mark us, he shall see
> Small change, when we're to bodies gone.

22. The references are to: "The Lotos-Eaters," "The Lady of Shalott," "Tithonus," "The Palace of Art," "Come Down, O Maid."
23. "Locksley Hall," 121-123.
24. The references are to Shakespeare in whom the parallel is a famous source of wordplay: "Hamlet," v, 2; "Two Gentlemen of Verona," ii, 4; "Richard II," iv, 1; "Cymbeline," ii, 5; "Othello," i, 2; "King John," ii, 1. And Carew speaking of Donne as enlightened by the "two flames" of poet and priest, refers to him as an "Exchequer" ("An Elegy upon the Death of the Dean of Paul's, Dr. John Donne," 43); similarly, E. A. Robinson on Shakespeare's "egregious shillings" in "Ben Jonson Entertains a Man from Stratford."
25. "Notes toward a Supreme Fiction," conclusion.
26. Cf. E. T. Dubois, *Portrait of Léon Bloy*, pp. 50-52.
27. Wallace Stevens, "Adagia," *Opus Posthumous*, p. 165.
28. Respectively, "The Fall of Hyperion," I, 13-15:

> Since every man whose soul is not a clod
> Hath visions, and would speak, if he had loved
> And been well-nurtured in his mother tongue.

And Wallace Stevens, "The Sense of the Sleight-of-hand Man," 1-3:

One's grand flights, one's Sunday baths,
One's tooting at the weddings of the soul
Occur as they occur.

29. In the radical definition, the prophet speaks *for* another;
whereas the person who predicts, merely speaks *before* the
event.
30. Respectively, "Why Did I Laugh Tonight?" 14; and "Ode
To a Nightingale," 52.
31. Psalm 22:6.
32. Crashaw, "Hymn of the Nativity," 79-84.
33. St. Thomas, *Summa Theologica*, I, 3, 3, ad. 2.
34. *Paradise Lost*, III, 380; and it is to the whole of the mystical
tradition of the Pseudo-Dionysius that Henry Vaughan is referring in "The Night," 49-50:

> There is in God (some say)
> A deep, but dazzling darkness.

35. *Une saison en enfer*, "L'impossible."
36. To embrace the antipodes is to encompass the entire world;
thus when the poet says, "wintry-warm" (Keats, "The Eve
of St. Agnes," 217-218), "manna-gall" (Donne, "Twicknam
Garden," —a typically Donnean play on the male and female
polarity), "Alps-Mecca" (Arnold, "Resignation: To Fausta,"
8, 3—an unArnoldian play on alpha-omega), he is attempting
to say *everything*, because there are no more ultimate extremities than spirit-matter.
37. "The Motive for Metaphor," 14-15.
38. Ralph Hodgson, "Eve," 29-30.
39. *Paradise Lost*, IV, 268-272; thus Milton to Charles Diodati
(In Patterson, *The Student's Milton*, p. 1080): "He [God] has
instilled into me, if into anyone, a vehement love of the
beautiful. Not with so much labor, as the fables have it, is
Ceres said to have sought her daughter Proserpina as it is
my habit day and night to seek for this idea of the beautiful, as for a certain image of supreme beauty, through all
the forms and faces of things (for many are the shapes of
things divine) and to follow it as it leads me on by some
sure traces which I seem to recognize."

40. Thus Gertrud von Le Fort, *Hymns to the Church*, "Corpus Christi Mysticum I":

> For we lay in the darkness of the Godhead one with another, we lay unawakened in the secret of the maker. Closer to one another than love, we were one before the dawn of creation.

41. For this reason Milton, *Paradise Lost*, IX, 395-6, compares Eve before the fall

> to Ceres in her Prime,
> Yet virgin of Proserpina from Jove.

Ceres is to Proserpine as Eve before the fall is to Eve after the fall, when she becomes the twilight maid in the world of the divided image.

42. Respectively, "Ode to a Nightingale," 67; "The Solitary Reaper," 3; "Kubla Khan," 22; "Elegy on the Death of the Dean of Paul's," 4; John 6: 35.

43. John 6:31.

44. "Hurrahing in Harvest," 5-6.

45. Respectively, "Kubla Khan," 11; "La Belle Dame Sans Mercy," 19; similarly for the oblique of poetry, "The valley of its saying" (Auden), "the valleys wild" (Blake), "in Tennessee ... upon a hill" (Stevens). References could be multiplied indefinitely.

46. Respectively, "Kubla Khan," 25; "Romanticism and Classicism," in Bate, *Criticism: The Major Texts*, p. 573: ". . . as the motion of a snake's body goes through all parts at once and its volition acts at the same instant in coils which go contrary ways."

47. *Paradise Lost*, IX, 510, 501; similarly, the "water snakes" in "The Rime of the Ancient Mariner," 278-280:

> Blue, glossy green, and velvet black
> They coiled and swam; and every track
> Was a flash of golden fire.

48. The obvious reason for so polarizing the colors into spirit-

matter, cool-warm (which represents their place in the spectrum) is that red and yellow are foreground colors, and unlike blue and green, do not seem to extend into infinity. Spengler supplies some ingenious historical parallels in *The Decline of the West*, I, pp. 246 ff. So too Lamia, serpent-woman and perfect poem, is described by Keats in *Lamia*, 47-48:

> She was a gordian shape of dazzling hue,
> Vermilion-spotted, golden, green, and blue.

49. "The Motive for Metaphor," 22, 14.
50. "The Tower," II, 30.
51. "Upon Phyllis Walking in a Morning before Sun-rising," 49-54.
52. "Hymn to God, My God in My Sickness," 26; "Hurrahing in Harvest," 10.
53. John 3: 14.
54. "The Rime of the Ancient Mariner," 615.
55. Similarly, Wallace Stevens, "Annual Gaiety," 5-6, finds the urge to poetry in the fact that "alligators lie along the edges of your eye"; the alligators are Mrs. Malaprop's allegories swimming in the sacred river. (And one muses on the fact that Uther Pen-dragon gave birth to that great king whose one supreme artifact, the round table, "was an image of the mighty world." Tennyson, "Morte d'Arthur," 235.)
56. "The Night," 3. This supplies another and different reason for the application to Christ of the words of the Psalm: "I am a worm and no man."
57. "Behold I have given you power to tread upon serpents." Luke 10: 19.
58. Respectively, "The Leaden Echo and the Golden Echo," 31; "The Hollow Men," 23; "Childe Roland to the Dark Tower Came," 182.
59. "Meditations in Time of Civil War," VI, 4: "My wall is loosening"; and, VII, 1: "I climb to the tower-top and lean upon broken stone."
60. "The Leaden Echo and the Golden Echo," 4.
61. Browning, "How it Strikes a Contemporary," 20-21.
62. Ephesians 2:20.

63. Acts 2: 8-12; and hence, too, the emphasis on the movement from multiplicity to unity in the epistle to the Hebrews 1: 1-2: "God who at sundry times and in divers manners spoke in times past to the fathers by the prophets, last of all in these days has spoken to us by his son."
64. In Griggs, *Unpublished Letters*, II, 128.
65. Isaiah 40: 4; Philippians 4: 7.
66. "Reason and Imagination," 5-7.
67. Galatians, 3: 9 ff.
68. Ephesians, 2: 14.
69. "Kubla Khan," 53-54.
70. *Paradise Lost*, IV, 28.
71. Auden, "Ode; To My Pupils," 13, 11.
72. Psalm 147: 15, Vulgate.
73. Antiphon for vespers in the Roman liturgy, December 17.
74. "For My Brother: Reported Missing in Action, 1943," 17-19:

> The money of Whose tears shall fall
> Into your weak and friendless hand
> And buy you back to your own land.

Similarly, Crashaw of the tears of the Magdalen ("Saint Mary Magdalene," 124-126):

> Waited on by a wandering mine,
> A voluntary mint, that strowes
> Warm silver showers where're he goes.

75. "Apology for Bad Dreams," IV, 2.
76. In Clark, *Home at Grasmere*, 241; similarly Keats in *Endymion* III, 56-58:

> Thou does bless every where, with silver lip
> Kissing dead things to life. The sleeping kine,
> Couched in thy brightness, dream of fields divine.

77. "The Leaden Echo and the Golden Echo," 27.
78. Respectively, "Immortality Ode," 72; "Resolution and Independence," 47.
79. Stevens, "Sunday Morning," VII, 4.

80. Respectively, Yeats, "Sailing to Byzantium," 24; Stevens, "Asides on the Oboe," 21; Stevens, "Sunday Morning," VII, 14-15; "On the Morning of Christ's Nativity," 135.
81. Isaiah, 52: 7; "Il Penseroso," 155. Compare *Comus*, 12-13.
82. Respectively, Isaiah 45: 8; Marvell, "On a Drop of Dew," 37-40.
83. John 6: 32-35.
84. "Asides on the Oboe," 2-3.
85. Yeats, "Among School Children," VII, 8; similarly, "The Tower," III, 44-45.
86. "The Motive for Metaphor," 17-19.
87. "The Tinker," 10-13; given the decline of Wordsworth's art, it is not surprising that he suppressed this poem.
88. "The Idea of Order at Key West," 26.
89. *Paradise Lost*, I, 740.
90. "The Tiger," 13-16.
91. "The Sense of the Sleight-of-hand Man," 19.
92. "One Word More," 74-77. The biblical text implied is I Cor. 10: 2-5.
93. Matthew 3: 9; John 4: 10.
94. Hebrews, 4: 12. This may be the reason both for Milton's bitter attack on poetry in *Paradise Regained*, IV, 285 ff., and for his elaborate self-ordination in the *Christian Doctrine*, where he affirmed that any believer was "competent to act as an ordinary minister" of the gospel, and that "extraordinary ministers" are persons inspired and sent on a special mission by God to reform the church "through the medium of preaching or of writing." (Chapters XXVIII and XXX)
95. "Lycidas," 123-131.
96. *Paradise Lost*, III, 139-140; 3.
97. John 12:30.
98. "The Motive for Metaphor," 16.
99. "Break, Break, Break," 15.
100. Donne, "The Good-morrow," 19-21, was speaking primarily of the metaphor of human love when he wrote:

What ever dies was not mixed equally
If our two loves be one, or thou and I
Love so alike, that none do slacken, none can die.

170

101. Stevens, "To the One of Fictive Music," 29.
102. "The Great Lover," 16.
103. "The Leaden Echo and the Golden Echo," 28.
104. Respectively, "The Ancient Mariner," 193; "The Bishop Orders His Tomb at Saint Praxed's Church," 113; "Tears, Idle Tears," 20; and so St. Paul (Romans, 14:9), "That was why Christ died and lived again; he would be Lord both of the dead and of the living." (Knox translation)
105. "Ode to a Nightingale," 8.
106. "Hymn to God, My God in My Sickness," 3.
107. "The Leaden Echo and the Golden Echo," 16-17:

> Despair, despair, despair, despair
> Spare!

108. Keats, "Hyperion," III, 126-130:

> Most like the struggle at the gate of death;
> Or liker still to one who should take leave
> Of pale immortal death, and with a pang
> As hot as death is chill, with fierce convulse
> Die into life.

109. Blake, "The Chimney Sweeper," 2-4:

> ...while yet my tongue
> Could scarcely cry " 'weep! 'weep! 'weep!"
> So your chimneys I sweep, and in soot I sleep.

But after the sweepers shall be released from their "coffins of black":

> Then down a green plain leaping, laughing, they run,
> And wash in a river, and shine in the sun.

110. Milton, "Lycidas," 17; "Begin, and somewhat loudly sweep the string."
111. Stevens, "The Motive for Metaphor," 1, 5.
112. "Twicknam Garden," 10.
113. Romans 6:4: "For we were buried with him by means of

baptism into death, in order that, just as Christ has arisen from the dead through the glory of the Father, so we also may walk in newness of life." This is implicitly the theme of Herbert's "Easter Wings," and explicitly of Vaughan's "The Waterfall"; and it is the "text" for the whole of the *The Waste Land*.

114. Cf. St. Justin Martyr, *First Apology*, chapter 61.
115. Wordsworth, "Tintern Abbey," 40.
116. "Ode on a Grecian Urn," 49-50.
117. Marvell, "The Garden," 51-56:

> Casting the body's vest aside,
> My soul into the boughs does glide:
> There like a bird it sits, and sings,
> Then whets and combs its silver wings;
> And, till prepared for longer flight,
> Waves in its plumes the various light.

# 2: Towards a Poetic of the Word

1. Originally a paper read at a meeting of the National Council on Religion in Higher Education.
2. *Criticism: The Major Texts*, ed. Walter Jackson Bate, New York, 1952, pp. 60-61.
3. *Critics and Criticism*, ed. R. S. Crane, Chicago, 1952, p. 93.
4. *An Essay in Aid of A Grammar of Assent*, New York, 1947, p. 72.
5. *Critics and Criticism*, p. 17.
6. *Ibid.*, p. 560.
7. *Ibid.*, p. 563.
8. Chicago, 1953, p. 15.
9. *Ibid.*, p. 248.
10. Blake, "Laughing Song," 5-8.
11. Yeats, "Among School Children," VI, 7-8.
12. Owen, "From My Diary, July, 1914."
13. Eliot, "Burnt Norton," V.
14. *Critics and Criticism*, p. 564.

15. Hopkins, "Pied Beauty," 7-8.
16. *The Verbal Icon*, New York, 1958, p. 5.
17. *The Well Wrought Urn*, New York, 1947, p. 204.
18. *Critics and Criticism*, pp. 54-55.
19. *The Man of Letters in the Modern World*, New York, 1955, p. 179.
20. Stevens, "Sunday Morning," VII, 14-15.
21. Yeats, "Prayer for My Daughter," X, 7-8.
22. Stevens, "Homunculus et La Belle Étoile," 25-32.
23. *Critics and Criticism*, p. 6.
24. Benedict Ashley, O. P., *The Arts of Learning and Communication*, Dubuque, 1958, p. 218.
25. Stevens, "Asides on the Oboe," II, 3-5.
26. Cf. G. S. Fraser, *Vision and Rhetoric*, New York, 1960, p. 66: "Now analysis is an admirable way of testing, and of reinforcing, summary judgments arrived at by ordinary literary tact and sensibility. It is not a substitute for tact and sensibility; it is not, and cannot be, the *primary* instrument of literary appreciation." (original italics)
27. John Henry Newman, *Autobiographical Writings*, New York, 1957, p. 150.
28. T. S. Eliot, *Notes Towards the Definition of Culture*, New York, 1947, p. 113.
29. Auden, "In Memory of W. B. Yeats," II, 5-7.
30. Stevens, "The Idea of Order at Key West," 44-51.
31. Blake, "The Little Black Boy," 15-16.
32. Blake, "The Echoing Green," 26-28.
33. *Lectures on the Prophetical Office of the Church*, London, 1837, pp. 108-109.
34. *Poems and Essays*, New York, 1955, p. 97.
35. Pope, "An Essay on Criticism," 311-312.
36. *Critics and Criticism*, p. 55.
37. Brooke, "The Chilterns," 36-40.
38. Wordsworth, "The Solitary Reaper," 9-16.
39. Cleveland, "On the Memory of Mr. Edward King, Drowned in the Irish Seas," 53-54.
40. Milton, "Lycidas," 155-157.
41. Coleridge, "The Rime of the Ancient Mariner," 109-110.
42. "What is a University?" *The Idea of a University*, Chicago, 1927, p. 471.

173

43. *Ways and Crossways*, New York, 1934, pp. 92-93, 95.
44. *Critics and Criticism*, p. 519.
45. *Aesthetics and History*, New York, 1948, p. 21.
46. *The Living God*, London, 1933, p. 238.
47. Stevens, "The Sense of the Sleight-of-hand Man," 1-3.

# 3: Poet, Metaphysician, and the Desire for God

1. The vision of Wordsworth on Westminster Bridge necessarily fades: it is only in the world of innocence that "heaven and earth to peace beguiles" (Blake, "A Cradle Song"), that the dualities are properly denominated as singular.
2. Keats, "Lamia," II, 234-237.
3. *The Necessary Angel*, New York, 1951, p. 59.
4. "The Idea of Order at Key West," *The Collected Poems of Wallace Stevens*, New York, 1961, p. 130. (Hereafter references to *Collected Poems* will be noted CP.)
5. "Evening without Angels," CP, p. 137.
6. "The Sense of the Sleight-of-hand Man," CP, p. 222.
7. *Ibid.*
8. E. E. Cummings, "La Guerre," II, 1-9.
9. W.B. Yeats, "The Tower," II, 30.
10. "Esthétique du Mal," CP, p. 320.
11. "Pieces," CP, p. 351.
12. "The Motive for Metaphor," CP, p. 228.
13. "Notes toward a Supreme Fiction," CP, p. 407.
14. "The Comedian as the Letter C," CP, p. 35.
15. "Idiom of the Hero," CP, p. 200.
16. "The Sense of the Sleight-of-hand Man," CP, p. 222.
17. "Adagia," *Opus Posthumous*, New York, 1957, p. 175. (Hereafter references to *Opus Posthumous* will be noted OP.)
18. "Last Look at the Lilacs," CP, p. 49.
19. "Rationalists, wearing square hats,/Think, in square rooms,/Looking at the floor,/Looking at the ceiling./They confine themselves/To right-angled triangles./If they tried rhom-

boids,/Cones, waving lines, ellipses—/As, for example, the ellipse of the half-moon—/Rationalists would wear sombreros." "Six Significant Landscapes," *CP*, p. 75.

20. "The Plot against the Giant," *CP*, p. 7.
21. "A Collect of Philosophy," *OP*, p. 185.
22. Of the historical Plato, Stevens wrote: "For Plato the only reality that mattered is exemplified best for us in the principles of mathematics." "On Poetic Truth," *OP*, p. 236.
23. It is to be noted that although "calm twilight" would have been rhythmically as effective, Keats stressed that this twilight has been *calmed* in order to bring out the presence of an operative power in this domain.
24. "De Idea Platonica," 37.
25. Despair hints at "spare" even as the *calmed* twilight hints at one who *calms*.
26. "In a world of universal poverty/ The philosophers alone will be fat...." "Like Decorations in a Nigger Cemetery," *CP*, p. 152.
27. "Sunday Morning," *CP*, p. 70.
28. Blake, "To the Evening Star," 10.
29. Cf. "Rorate Caeli" of the Roman Christmas liturgy.
30. "Sunday Morning," *CP*, p. 67.
31. "Anecdote of the Jar," *CP*, p. 76.
32. "Sunday Morning," *CP*, p. 68.
33. "The Man with the Blue Guitar," *CP*, p. 165.
34. "The adherents of the imagination are mystics to begin with and pass from one mysticism to another. The adherents of the central are also mystics to begin with. But all their desire and all their ambition is to press away from mysticism toward that ultimate good sense which we term civilization." *The Necessary Angel*, p. 116.
35. Hopkins, "The Leaden Echo and the Golden Echo."
36. Milton, "Lycidas," 143, 151.
37. The clasping of hands which signifies the union of heaven and earth, in the true salem-peace-pact, is achieved only by the poet when his miming music is joined to the music of the other world, when "... with fingers interwoven, both hands/ Pressed closely palm to palm, and to his mouth/ Uplifted, he, as through an instrument,/ Blew mimic hootings to the silent owls,/ That they might answer him;/ ... and that un-

certain heaven, received/ Into the bosom of the steady lake."
Wordsworth, "The Prelude," V, 370 ff.

38. Milton, "Il Penseroso," 63-64.
39. "Sunday Morning," *CP*, pp. 69-70.
40. Donne, "Hymne to God my God, in my sicknesse," 1-6:

> Since I am comming to that Holy roome,
>     Where, with thy Quire of Saints for evermore
> I shall be made thy Musique; As I come
>     I tune the instrument here at the dore,
>     And what I must doe then, thinke here before.

Schiller's "Ode to Joy," as set in the Ninth Symphony, fulfills this same function: the failure of the instrumental music
(*diese Toene*), and the need for it to be joined to the great
heavenly choral.

41. *Insight. A Study of Human Understanding*, New York, 1957,
    p. 656.
42. Joseph Maréchal, *Studies in the Psychology of the Mystics*,
    New York, 1927, p. 134.
43. "Laughing Song," 8.


# 4: The Dawn of the Sacred

1. Père C. J. Dumont, *La Vie Spirituelle*, January, 1950.
2. Preface to *The Art-Principle of the Liturgy*, trans. William
   Busch, Collegeville, Minn., 1931, p. vi. I have indicated other
   examples of this reciprocity in early Christian history in "The
   Splendor of the Chant," *Orate Fratres*, November, 1947.
3. I have discussed at greater length the inculcation of this sense
   of reverence in "The Christian Formation of Youth," *The
   Christian Imagination*, Westminster, Md., 1955.
4. Ia, 1, 9 ad 3.
5. Throughout the rest of this essay I will be speaking only of
   the liturgical arts as such; such adjectives as sacred, religious,
   liturgical, and Christian will be used interchangeably to describe this art.
6. *L'Art Sacré*, April, 1950.

7. *L'Art Sacré*, June, 1950.
8. "... one certainly does not lessen the dignity of art by point-ing out, around its highest masterpieces, the faint aureola of a missed holiness. Art is good in itself; perfect art is perfect in itself, but it has nothing to lose from being kept in its proper place." Etienne Gilson, *Measure*, The Henry Regnery Co., Chicago, 1950.
9. Claudel's dialogue between the Chaplain and the Viceroy teaches its own lesson here. The Chaplain remarks that he would not have thought Rubens a preacher of the Gospel; to which the Viceroy replies: "And who then has better glori-fied Flesh and Blood than Rubens, that very flesh and blood in which a God decreed to clothe Himself and which became the instrument of our redemption. It is said that the stones themselves will cry out! Is it only to the human body that you would deny speech!" *The Satin Slipper*, Paris, 1929, I, 150.
10. I would take as a symbol of this the two typically romantic murals of Delacroix in the chapel of the Church of St. Sulpice. Considering the fidelity of the Sulpicians to the theological doctrine of the French School with its contempt for the human body and its disdain for all that is purely human in Christ, one might have expected these paintings to reflect this doctrine. That the painter pursued his own in-tuitions, rather than abstract theology, has resulted in works which are, by that very fact, more profoundly artistic *and* theological.
11. The London *Tablet*, December 2, 1950.
12. *Art-making from Mexico to China*, Jean Charlot, New York, 1950.

# 5: The Christian Themes of Marc Chagall

1. *The Decline of the West*, New York, 1926, p. 294.
2. Quoted in, *From Picasso to Surrealism*, New York, 1950, p. 112.
3. New York, 1960, p. 39.

# INDEX OF NAMES

179

# Date Due

| DE 3 '69 | | | | | |
|---|---|---|---|---|---|
| JUL 29 '69 | | | | | |
| DEC 21 '79 | | | | | |
| | | | | | |
| | | | | | |
| | | | | | |
| | | | | | |
| | | | | | |
| | | | | | |